COMMUNITY DEVELOPMENT: EDUCATION AND TRAINING IN THEORY AND PRACTICE

Paschal W Odoch

MINERVA PRESS

LONDON
MONTREUX   LOS ANGELES   SYDNEY

COMMUNITY DEVELOPMENT: EDUCATION AND TRAINING IN THEORY AND PRACTICE

ISBN 1 86106 768 2

First Published 1997 by
MINERVA PRESS
195 Knightsbridge
London SW7 1RE

Printed in Great Britain for Minerva Press

COMMUNITY DEVELOPMENT: EDUCATION AND TRAINING IN THEORY AND PRACTICE

To my wife, Juliet, and our children

Acknowledgements

First and foremost my sincere appreciation goes to my supervisors for their promptness and effective guidance in the course of developing this study. Dr Tom Sork has been thoughtful and responsive in the effort to pursue the study conclusively. Utmost thanks is extended to Dr Hillel Goelman, for having augmented the study as a second reader.

A special appreciation is extended to people whose participation and co-operation made this study possible. DISSA members, in particular, the group Co-ordinator Garbet Alichan, who made available the project documents; sub-unit Managers – James Wathum and Jenaro Onegi, who co-ordinated the completion and timely mailing of the survey questionnaire; and the group Secretary, Caesar Kachungumbe, for having provided the programme photographs.

Equally appreciated are the following who shared with me academic and informal subjects with implications for the study; my 'old' colleagues from Uganda, Lesotho and graduate colleagues from Simon Fraser University and the University of British Columbia. More personally, I am thankful to Dr Stephen Ameyaw at Community Economic Development Centre, Simon Fraser University, John C. Rhoad Jr, and Steve Collision for their excellent views. Finally, I am indebted to my family for having had the patience as well as providing me with moral support throughout the study period. To all these people I say the conclusion of the study is the beginning of the actual work of meeting the challenges of human resource development.

I acknowledge the general administrative and other assistance rendered to me by the Adult Education Research Centre, University of British Columbia. Without the support this study would not have been a reality.

About the Author

    Paschal Wathum Odoch was born on March 31, 1966, at the Angal Missionary Hospital in the Nebbi district of Uganda. He was educated at Nyapea College, Nebbi; Busoga College, Mwiri, Jinja, and Makerere University where he obtained BA Hons in Economics and Social Administration in 1990. He proceeded to work as Organisation and Methods Officer at the Ministry of Public Service and Cabinet Affairs, Entebbe, before taking up a job as Principal of Masianokeng Commercial Community School in Lesotho for two years. Mr Odoch holds a Graduate Diploma in Community Economic Development from Simon Fraser University, Burnaby (1994), and a M.Ed. in Adult Education form the University of British Columbia, Canada (1996). Among other things, Mr Odoch has consulted with the Public Participation Branch of the Canadian International Development Agency (CIDA). At the time of publication, Mr Odoch is the Executive Director of the Program for Appropriate Community Technology (PACT), a Vancouver-based Canadian non-governmental organisation engaged in the promotion of local level community development in sub-Saharan Africa.

Preface

Few things have been more clearly demonstrated during the past twenty years than the fact that overall benefits of conventional advanced technologies (which are typically large-scale, very expensive, labour-saving, capital and energy intensive), have not trickled down to the great majority of the poor in the developing world. The existing technological deficiency coupled with the low level of investment in human resources have resulted in an inequitable form of development, where the rural and urban poor (who comprise the great majority of the developing world's population), are bypassed. It is therefore not surprising that development aspirations of these countries with regard to improving the quality of life of rural and urban poor have not been adequately met. Amidst this impoverishment, the life support systems of the poor continue to be traditional, based on family and community networks. Main economic activities are on a small scale, with barter and subsistence playing a major role. Thus, a great majority of these people continue to live in an informal rather than the formal economy. Moreover it is the informal sector of the economy that is unappreciated by public policy makers.

In view of the above, the idea that development starts with the people, and assists them in what they aim at achieving, becomes more important in policy process. Based on this understanding, it is my conviction that a single factor which strengthens development initiatives in the community is the creation of a climate that fosters active involvement of people. The process of establishing this climate includes getting into the community in question, collaboratively discovering local needs, and creating methods that meet those needs.

This study sets to explore DISSA, an integrated community development initiative (in Uganda from late 1980s) with regard to the process and strategy applied in the mobilisation of the community for effective socio-political and economic participation and development.

Contents

I   Introduction   13

II   Models and Principles of Community Development   16

     Models for Community Development   17
     Central Ideas and Expressions of Community
     Development   19
     Community Development and Learning Process   26
     Traditional Approaches to Community Development   29
     Conclusion   32

III   Community Development In Practice   35

     Uganda: An Historical Overview   35
     DISSA Community Development Initiative   37
     Project Background   40
     Project Organisation and Activities   42
     Implementation   44
     Linkages   48
     Impact Assessment   49
     Impediments   54
     Analysis   55
     Conclusion   63

IV   Community Development Training and Education   65

     Training Approach for Community Development   67
     Importance of the Training Design   70
     Planning and Management of Community Development   71
     Implementation Process for Community Development   74
     Monitoring Community Development Initiatives   76
     Evaluation of Community Development Initiatives   77
     Community Development and Further Investigation   80

V   Conclusion   82

Appendix A: Survey Questionnaire   85

Appendix B: Figures   93

    Figure 1
    Map showing the Location of Uganda within Africa   94

    Figure 2
    Map of Uganda showing Administrative Boundaries   95

    Figure 3
    Map of Northern Uganda showing DISSA's
    Nebbi district   96

    Figure 4
    DISSA Management Flow Chart   97

Appendix C: Table I   99

    Distribution of Tribes in Uganda   100

References   101

Chapter I

Introduction

Community development programs have been initiated and implemented in many African countries, either by governments or private organisations. Sautoy (1962), a pioneer in African community development, asserts in the preface to his book that, while the principles of community development are comparatively simple to understand, it is the application of the principles which presents the most difficulty. In 1960, the Cambridge Conference on African Administration stressed the importance of training and educating people to become agents for change in order to improve their own living conditions. Consequently, the United Nations Report (1971) identified a broad range of undertakings that fit under the umbrella term 'community development'. In the report, two elements stand out: (i) efforts by people themselves to improve their conditions and (ii) community assistance from government to facilitate the achievement of goals. In a community development initiative, training is essential in bridging theory and practice to programme implementation. Furthermore, in considering that community development aims to institute social change, it is appropriate to conclude that education, training and organisational initiatives are imperative.

The purpose of this book is to argue that the most appropriate vehicles for facilitating sustainable community development processes are trained practitioners and community members, who then actively participate in implementing community projects.

In the book, community development is defined as a "process by members of a community, however defined, determine to take stock of their community, set goals for desirable change, and work towards those goals" (Elias & Merriam, 1980: p.9). In this process, learning is a bridge-point[1]. Community development also means a process by which the efforts of people themselves are united with those of non-governmental authorities to improve the social and cultural conditions of communities, to integrate these communities into the life of the nation, and to enable them to contribute fully to national progress (United Nations, 1971; Wileden, 1970).

The book's second chapter presents models of community development, a literature review, and an overview of the principles that guide community development programs. Implications of the models and principles are explored and an interface developed between the models and community development practice. Established works in adult education that are linked to community development initiatives are examined including social action, collective action, consciousness raising and transformative learning. Because of the highly complex nature of the community development concept, the book identifies principles that are embraced by many community development initiatives.

The third chapter explores the strategy and methods applied for mobilising community and resources in the Displaced Students' Association (DISSA), an adult/youth development initiative in Uganda, East Africa. Through this community development experience, the book draws a relationship between the central ideas and processes of community development and initiatives which utilise adult education and training to achieve their goals. The book develops a body of work on DISSA largely from the responses in the survey questionnaire (refer to Appendix A) that was mailed (from Vancouver to Uganda) to DISSA executive committee members during the course of study. The Project Appraisal Memorandum (PAM, 1992) made available by DISSA management provided supplementary information to the book. DISSA development initiative is located in a locality where the author was born and lived until 1990 when he took a job assignment in Maseru (Lesotho) and later in 1992 to Canada to pursue further studies. The author's familiarity and knowledge about the geography, people and the politics of the region provides an insider perspective and insights to the background description of the DISSA

---

[1] It is further stressed that "there is a great deal of learning on the part of those involved, about the state of the community, its actions, the range of options available, and the management of the group processes involved in all these efforts." (Elias & Merriam 1980:p.9).

development initiative. The chapter further examines the entire process (from inception to project implementation) that was carried out by DISSA in achieving their goals. The analysis section features DISSA integrated community development project within the purview of the central ideas and principles of community development. The goal of this analysis is to broaden an understanding of *what works* and *what does not work* in a community development initiative of this magnitude. The author postulates that the results of the book could be applied to most other community development initiatives with similar characteristics, problems and potential. The analysis is structured so that central ideas and principles of community development are in the normal font while DISSA's approach is featured in italics.

Chapter Four addresses community development training and education. The author argues that development co-ordinators should be skilled in both community development and project management techniques in order to serve as a link between self-help community development initiatives and public institutions. Covered in detail is the training approach (implicit in DISSA) for community development planning and management, the target groups for training, and an examination of the training design concept. Desired methods of monitoring and evaluating the training programs in particular and for community development initiatives in general are described. The final chapter explores the type of research that should be conducted so as to better understand planning at the community level.

Chapter II
Models and Principles of Community Development

This chapter presents a review of community development literature and concludes with models and principles of what are useful for understanding community development initiatives. Through this process the author aims to summarise the principles which guide many community development programs in Third World environments.

In most parts of sub-Sahara[2] Africa, people have played major development roles in their respective rural communities. In Kenya, for example, a study by Nelson (1979) notes that women brewers from the Mathare Valley rely on mutual aid groups for wholesale buying and selling of raw-corn. Similar research in Lesotho by Allan, Carmichael, Karimjee (1993), reveal that challenges facing communities had to be resolved by the active involvement of the Mohale's Hoek community. Raynor and Harden (1973), argue that it is through community-based education and training that community members acquire the necessary knowledge, understanding and skills to interpret and improve their environment. Kauzeni (1990), for example, stresses that training and planning approaches, environmental problem-solving techniques, involvement of local people and integrated resource management are vital for sustaining local-level development initiatives. Bibi (1990), argues that training should be provided to local leaders in successfully managing projects in their own communities. Kauzeni (1990) and Ameyaw (1989), both agree that

---

[2] Sub-Sahara Africa is a geo-political term that denotes the countries on the African Continent, south of the Sahara desert and north of the Limpopo River in southern Africa. Despite its richness in both cultural diversity and cultivable soils (and where most of its inhabitants are sedentary pastoralists and crop producers), the zone is plagued by challenges of social development due to a lack of vast mineral deposits as compared to the northern and southern fringes of the continent.

training of human resources from the local community should be given high priority in any community development initiative.

Eight major programme planning models that deal with processes relevant to adult education and training place emphasis on the design component (Beal et al, 1966; Boone, 1971; Boyle, 1981; Houle, 1972; Kidd, 1973; Knowles, 1970; Sork, 1994; Tyler, 1949). Therefore, the encouragement and promotion of participatory local-level planning and development designs in rural communities (which account for more than eighty per cent of most of developing economies' population), is a potentially useful way of improving the lot of people with incomes below the poverty line (UNCRD, 1992).

Models for Community Development

As a grass-roots based and directed process that explicitly combines socio-cultural and economic aspects, community development strives to foster the economic, social, ecological and cultural well-being of its members and regions. It is founded on the belief that contemporary problems facing communities – unemployment, poverty, job loss due to economic restructuring and economic instability, environmental degradation and loss of community control– need to be addressed in a holistic and participatory way. Williams (1987) and Dauncey (1988) provide models for understanding community development initiatives that are consistent with these beliefs. Williams perceptively discerns two potentially conflicting approaches emerging. The first is based on community participation and attempts to blend economic factors with broader social issues. From this viewpoint, community development is considered as an integrated set of programmes that address social, environmental, cultural and economic issues[3]. In contrast to this holistic approach to community development is what Williams terms the business school approach, which views community development as essentially an economic programme. This approach sets increased employment opportunities as community development goals, and entrepreneurship as the strategy. Williams regards this approach as becoming institutionalised in most government-initiated programmes

---

[3] Applications of this approach include The Uganda Women's Finance and Credit Trust, the West Acholi Co-operative Union, the Busoga Multi-sectoral Rural Development Programme, and ActionAid Mityana Programme (de Coninck, 1992).

because it is more understandable and attractive to those who control start-up funds.

Dauncey, however, presents a more complex view of community development. He identifies six models of development, namely, top-down macro-economic management, smoke-stack chasing, local economic development, community economic development, organisational transformation, and planetary transformation. His first and second models are termed the growth promotion approach to community development. The third and fourth models are congruent with what is termed the structural change approach to community development. And the fifth and sixth models parallel a communalisation approach.

In examining Dauncey's models, the most compelling are local economic development and community economic development. Both these models embrace the central ideas and principles that form the blocks of community development, namely: a) the models embrace a holistic view to policy formulation as they accommodate the views of different groups in the community (Selman & Dampier, 1991; Hume, 1993). They both recognise the functional interconnections between economic and social problems and produce initiatives that address every aspect of their impacts on the community (Moron, 1983); b) that community-based development initiatives are well connected to the communities in which they operate (Knowles, 1980; Hodge and Qadeer, 1983; Dykeman, 1988). By implication, they are better able to mobilise local resources over the long-term as well as recognising development potentials that are not obvious to outside investors; and c) they both foster community identity with a development initiative. This reinforces the notion where communities view development initiatives as programmes *by us – for us* rather than *by them – for us* (Christenson & Jerry, 1989; Littrell &, 1989; Fear, Gamm & Fisher, 1989).

Since the 1930s, community development has taken various forms in order to increase people's participation in local development initiatives, raise production and standards of living, enhance participation in the work force and achieve self-determination (Dykeman, 1988). Furthermore, whatever forms community development took, especially during the last five decades, and irrespective of the social, political, economic and cultural factors it emphasised, the notion itself has consistently embraced the central ideas and principles adopted by its practitioners.

Central Ideas and Expressions of Community Development

Given the variety of ideas central to community development, developed either alone or in combination with others, by practitioners, groups or agencies from often different backgrounds and ideologies, what arises is interpretation in an even greater variety of expressions[4], depending on the interests and priorities of the users in the context of the social, political and economic situation of the time. It is therefore challenging to make a complete list of all forms and expressions community development can take. However, authorities in the field of community development do suggest a classification of community development approaches that is useful to this book.

COMMUNITY DEVELOPMENT AS A PROCESS

Advocates of this approach pursue process goals rather than target goals. This approach aims to mobilise community members into action groups in order to respond to issues and problems that concern them. Depending on the situation or need, this process may utilise self-help, mutual aid or social action. Typical cases are group development, leadership development, organisation and management development and inter-group relations (Christenson & Jerry, 1989; Lotz, 1971; Compton 1971).

COMMUNITY DEVELOPMENT AS A METHOD

Community development as a methodology is concerned with the performance of individuals, groups and organisations in the context of their community. Common strategies used include: community organising, group work, adult education and demonstrations. In more sophisticated societies, other specialised fields are also used (e.g., planning, law, politics and finance), (Knowles, 1980; Lotz 1971; Compton 1971).

---

[4] Drawn from the British Columbia Provincial and Follow-up Meeting on Community Economic Development Document (1992).

COMMUNITY DEVELOPMENT AS INSTITUTIONAL INITIATIVE

This form of community development came into prominence after World War II and took either the form of political movements (India) or was placed under the jurisdiction of various government ministries as a way of mobilising the masses for raising the standard of living (Ujamaa in Tanzania), attacking illiteracy (South America) or broadening general participation in the work force. Typical forms include social service non-governmental organisations, environmental organisations and community social planning organisations. The organisations are solidly based on the "bottom-up" principle and through community co-ordinators' roles, participation of the community members in goal attainment is fostered, (Hume, 1993; Christenson & Jerry, 1989; Warner, 1989).

COMMUNITY DEVELOPMENT AS SOCIAL MOVEMENT

As a movement, community development is expressed in the form of self-help groups, co-operatives, community associations and community economic development.

It also features in such forms as: a) decentralisation of government or non-governmental organisational structures. In this case, the primary concern is for enabling "left-out" groups to accede to greater degree of control, planning and decision-making over resources and services, while simultaneously encouraging the decision makers to deliver services more responsibly to meet local needs (Compton, 1971); b) citizen participation, which occurs not when tolerated, encouraged or even decreed, but only when citizens recognise it as meaningful and effective on their terms; c) self-help groups based on mutual-aid, controlled by peers and normally engaged in goal-directed activities, (Draper, 1971; OECD, 1985); d) community associations that organise and aim at gaining greater control over their own life through full or partial ownership of resources. Strategies used include the establishment of community-based service centres, leadership training, fund-raising and social action (Stinson, 1979); e) co-operatives which abide by their fundamental principles of democratic control, open membership, limited interest on share capital, proportional distribution of profits and promotion of education. Co-operatives are in themselves, vivid expressions of community development institutions (Dykeman, 1989; Littrell & Hobbs, 1989); f) community economic development, with its roots in the co-operative movement, involves a number of people as self-governing groups, but aims at embarking on new forms of profit-making enterprises for the socio-economic benefit of the members of the community. The aim is to work closely with marginalised groups, drawing on idle resources and free labour, and to combine those resources with capital investment in order to address social problems faced.

Whatever form community development initiatives take, there are common elements that are shared and ones which facilitate their classification under the umbrella term – community development. The elements include active participation, self-reliance and community control, consciousness-raising and empowerment, capacity building, co-operation and collaboration and community self-evaluation.

PARTICIPATION

Community development encourages the active participation of all members of the community in planning, decision-making and works to remove the barriers that limit participation of its citizens. In particular, community development seeks to encourage the active participation of women, youth, seniors, ethnic groups, and indigenous peoples in the public life of the community.

Beal et al (1966) present a perspective on planning that is sociological and social system oriented. In their view, a cautiously planned and built consensus is vital for any community programme. That participation is advocated through selected terminology appropriately applied (i.e., initiating sets – those who get the idea moving) and commitment of the community members to goal attainment. Thus, an agreement has to be reached by the very community who stand to benefit from any initiative.

The Boone et al (1971) approach to planning is designed in the context of community development extension work. As an outgrowth of Beal et al, a unique element they bring to planning from an educational perspective is the notion of group work. They argue that the educator (in this case the community development co-ordinator), should have a commitment to programming that links the organisation and its community members through needs analysis and leader involvement. Although participation is not directly mentioned in the model, a participatory planning process is implicit in the conceptual schema. This is a view supported by Freire (1970) in his approach to planning and programming. To Freire, participation is a central construct in the entire planning process. This is clearly illustrated where he argues "adult literacy programme is an act of knowledge and creativity by which learners function along with educators as knowing subjects" (Freire, 1985: p. 102). In Freire's view, through problem posing, community members are made to think critically and develop a form of action to address a situation so identified. Accommodating the interests of all members in a community, including women, youth, the elderly, the mentally and physically challenged, minority groups, can through this reflexive pattern and problem posing process be reflected in all aspects of community planning and actions (Compton, 1971; Roberts, 1979).

SELF-RELIANCE AND LOCAL COMMUNITY CONTROL

Community development builds on local strengths, creativity and resources. It actively seeks to decrease dependency on, and vulnerability to, economic interests outside of the community or region. Furthermore, community development supports decentralised, non-hierarchical decision-making processes thereby strengthening the autonomy of the individual, the community and the region.

Sustainable community development must come from the "bottom-up" that is, from within the community (Ross & Usher, 1986). The development plan and initiative should reflect the community's chosen future direction (e.g., establishing a food processing plant) and indicate public or private sector responsibility for project implementation. The plan should be prepared from community primary data thereby providing first-hand and comprehensive guidance for the local development planning process. The initiatives should be realistic, make optimal use of existing community resources, and present demonstrable benefits over the long-term to the community (Seasons, 1988; Fenn, 1989).

CONSCIOUSNESS-RAISING AND EMPOWERMENT

At the most pro-active level, community development planning helps communities determine and organise their own services. Contracting out and decentralising community services has meant that more services are locally managed. Collective planning can help communities to determine how existing resources can best be used, and can assist those most affected by social issues to determine their own solutions (Draper, 1971; Robert, 1979; Forsey, 1993). Community development planning requires the establishment of a step-by-step process which allows the community to envision its own long term goals and objectives. Educational initiatives and consciousness-raising enable communities to manage the rate of social and cultural change and, more importantly, act appropriately (Uma, 1975; Cernea, 1983). Beal et al (1966) have alluded to this view by their approach to standard steps of goal setting, means of action, plans of action, resource mobilisation and action stages. In their view, the goal of consciousness-raising and empowerment are fostered through diffusion sets (the persons who spread the word). In a related construct, under their assumptions, Boone et al (1971) consider the adult educator as a change agent and programmer. They proceed to argue that a commitment and understanding of the philosophy, objectives, roles and relationships of the community organisation is imperative for instituting an awareness-raising amongst its members. Similarly, consciousness-raising as an educational and empowerment goal is a central construct in Freire's (1970) approach to planning. Freire affirms a process of decoding whereby participants interpret the themes individually and in the process, make explicit their real consciousness of the world. Applied to his literacy training programme, Freire argues that it is in this learning process that actual codification occurs, and is built around words and pictures. By separating the "generative words" into syllables, the students are then led to create other words using these syllables and their symbol families. As they begin to write brief notes, they continue to discuss and analyse critically the real context represented in the codification. Freire further believes that participants begin to see how they themselves act while actually experiencing a situation they would analyse later. Through the broadened horizon of their perceptions, Freire argues that a discovery of dialectical relations between the two dimensions of reality (one's own definition as opposed to a definition by other people) is established.

CAPACITY BUILDING

Community development contributes to self-reliance by encouraging the acquisition of relevant skills and the development of supportive structures and institutions. It encompasses design of training programmes and the creation of structures and institutions to serve the needs of the community as well as fostering more productive use of available resources. Capacity building which is in part achieved through education and training, requires a plan designed to meet the specific needs of a community (OECD, 1985; UNCRD, 1992).

Beal et al (1966) utility of diffusion sets facilitate the process of spreading the word. Education of the community thus facilitates this process. Boone et al (1971) consider an educational framework as essential in defining and organising the learning activities in community extension work. To these authors, the role of the educator is key to programming in co-operative extension (educational) work. With more emphasis on educational needs and learning objectives, the goal of capacity building is clearly illuminated. Furthermore, the educator (in this case the community development co-ordinator) has an understanding of and skills in staffing, staff development, supervision, evaluation and accountability. Of the authors within a community-based setting and with regard to capacity building, Freire (1970) is perhaps the most outstanding. Through his concept of *banking education*, Freire criticised education for domestication and advocates a form of education that fosters critical reflection and thinking and not one that is designed to fill empty vessels with knowledge.

CO-OPERATION AND COLLABORATION

Community development recognises that there are important linkages and connections both within communities, between communities and regions, and that many problems cannot be addressed in isolation (Hodge & Qadeer, 1983). For instance, not every community can afford, nor do they all need, an industrial water pump, expensive marketing campaigns or an in-house economic development co-ordinator. Therefore, inter-community linkages need to be fostered and co-ordinated in areas of resource management and utilisation and alternative economic activities. The involvement of all levels of government and public institutions to provide support in the form of extension services, enabling legislation and avenues for rational capital funding are important to achieving desired community goals (Christenson & Jerry, 1989; Head, 1988).

In addition to the above discussion, Scott & Summers (1974) and Lassey (1977) suggest that co-operation and complementary resources should be encouraged among communities (e.g. the attraction of investment to benefit adjacent communities equally) and between public and private sector organisations. There is a need for close communication among communities and between levels of government to maximise opportunities and minimise problems that often arise from poorly defined policy direction. Thus, an improved inter-agency co-ordination in skills development and training is necessary to create a clear picture and understanding of a region's socio-economic (existing and potential) levels of development (Uma, 1975; Warner, 1989).

MONITORING AND EVALUATION

The community development process of monitoring and evaluation plays an important role in helping local service agencies, service providers and funders to consult with users of services (Christenson & Jerry, 1989). This helps ensure accountability to and evaluation by local communities where the service or programme is being provided (Steiner, 1979; Lang, 1988; Seasons, 1988; Filion, 1988). Without a local service role, it is difficult for programmes and services to be planned to effectively respond to local community priorities.

In describing their social action model (where feedback-loops are a major constituent), Beal et al (1966) establish a point for all programming tasks in which evaluation is considered an ongoing, continual process. At every one of the steps the authors outline in the model, great emphasis is placed on whether the original objectives were achieved and then, what next step to follow based on the evaluated target objective. Thus, these micro-loops are depicted as occurring at every level of development of social action programmes. Very much related to the Beal et al approach, is Freire's (1970) who regards evaluation as continuous. To these authors, evaluation is built into the programming process as a constant review of both information and perceptions about the community problem identified. Boone et al (1966) address evaluation from the perspective of the individual learner, and target public and organisational implications of both intended and unintended outcomes. The authors proceed to argue that even when planned change is adequately attained, evaluation has a broader application and mandate.

This section has examined the various forms of community development. Also discussed were the elements that are shared by all forms of community development initiatives and ones which ensure their classification under the umbrella term – community development. It is essential to state that the elements of community development discussed above (participation, self-reliance and community control, consciousness-raising and empowerment, capacity building, co-operation and collaboration and evaluation) are the most important[5]. Although mutually exclusive but not exhaustive, the elements indicate from a practical viewpoint some of the beliefs, values and processes of community development as derived from the literature.

Community Development and Learning Process

From a variety of ideas central to community development advanced by practitioners, groups or agencies, often from different backgrounds and ideologies, it is common to find an even greater variety of expressions, depending on the interests and priorities of the users in the context of the existing social, political and economic situation. It is the context that dictates the form of learning in a specific community development situation.

The process approach applied to community development initiatives aims particularly at mobilising community members into action groups in order to tackle issues and problems that concern them (Roberts, 1979). This is a view shared by Selman & Dampier (1991) who argue that, in the process of community development, active involvement by the beneficiary is key, especially about knowledge of the state of the community, the goals which can be agreed upon, the resources available to assist the community in its actions, the range of options available and the management of the group process involved in all these efforts.

Depending on the situation or need, the process approach is implicit in the notion of self-help, mutual aid and social action. Included in the approach is a focus on leadership development (i.e., the process that develops individual's confidence and skills to deal with relations between members, leading towards the group assuming its own

---

[5] According to the British Columbia Working Group on Community Economic Development (1992), other principles are: Equity; Community Building; Integration; Independence; Living Within Ecological Limits; Capacity Building; Diversity; and Application of Appropriate Indicators.

leadership) (Christenson & Jerry, 1989). This situation is upheld by the constructivist viewpoint, developed from constructivist philosophy (Von Glasersfeld, 1988) and advocates the application of cognitive psychology to curriculum (Champagne & Klopfer, 1984; Resnick, 1987). All of these authors emphasise the dynamic role of the learner in constructing interpretations of experience based on adaptive responses to the environment (community). In the case where an extension or outreach programme is conducted, a technique where learners acquire the new skills of practice while reflecting and interpreting such skills in the context of the challenge faced by the community is more desirable (Resnick, 1987).

A primary objective of action learning is to ensure that participants realise they can take initiatives based on interpretations of their own situation. This perspective is further supported by Candy (1991) who argues that becoming knowledgeable involves acquiring the symbolic meaning structures appropriate to one's community. Through the process of sharing information, appropriate knowledge is constructed and community members add or alter their existing knowledge base. The process of exchanging meanings and methods of community development initiatives is achieved through participants' knowledge construction based on the new information (from other successfully conducted initiatives), thereby fitting their own context.

In their notion of legitimate peripheral participation, Lave and Wenger (1991) argue that through an interactive process, the apprentices (in this context, the community development workers) are engaged through a simultaneous performance of several roles-status namely, as subordinates, learning practitioners and aspiring experts. Each of these roles implies a different form of responsibility, relations, and involvement. This process provides an opportunity for community participants to observe and integrate their accumulated knowledge and experience with the new techniques presented before proceeding to replicate them in their own community. Lave and Wenger (1991) further explore the character of human understanding and communication. They argue that human understanding takes a focus on the relationship between learning and the situation in which it occurs. This implies a highly interactive and productive utilisation of the skills that are acquired through the learning process. Via this process, a community participant does not acquire a discrete body of abstract knowledge which is transported and applied in a specific context. This central concept is useful for developing techniques and practical approaches that are transferred to communities that would later actively pursue their own community development initiatives.

A central tenet in the community development process is ensuring its members translate their thinking into collective action. In agreeing with this notion, Griffin (1981) argues that education for social action should achieve a personal transformation and collective social action. Mezirow (1990) discusses further that the adult educator (change agent) should be a role model who encourages others to consider approaches to the one being undertaken. This suits the situation of transferring skills and knowledge regarding how other community organisations successfully achieve their development goals. Based on participants' self insights, the role of the adult educator is to encourage such a desire for other community groups to change their way of practice. It should be pointed out that although the above is a logical argument and therefore socio-economically viable, it is not an absolute approach to community development aware of its diversity.

Community development as a method is concerned with the functioning of individuals, groups and organisations in the context of community. Common strategies applied include community social organisations, adult education and group work. These strategies are supported by Freire (1970) who demonstrated the possibilities of using education to bring about transformative learning among illiterate and semi-illiterate people. To Freire, conscientisation involves a group of people looking beyond their personal histories to the collective history of their group, their culture and class. In relating this phenomenon to community development initiatives, working together establishes credibility for the dynamic leader or 'spark plug' (i.e., a traditional chief or Mayor of a town who initiates, co-ordinates and gets things moving). The plan and programme that is developed through sharing knowledge and experience amongst community members reinforces the viability and longevity of the development initiative. This is a view shared by Houle (1972), who describes education as a co-operative venture, in which the role of a teacher is that of a facilitator.

Mezirow (1990) provides an understanding that action is an integral and indispensable component of transformative learning. To Mezirow, taking action that results from critical reflection may be impeded by lack of information or the absence of required skills. This interpretation is significant for communities that may be facing challenges, yet lacking the necessary information with which to make the needed undertaking. This phenomenon has implications for a wide range of organisations, including adult skills training, community development groups, environmental action groups, and other interest groups that attempt to institute change. It would also have implications for social service community organisations attempting to foster consciousness-raising and the promotion of broad-based alliances in support of peoples' welfare.

Traditional Approaches to Community Development

Communities in sub-Sahara African countries (including the ones examined in this book) have regarded community development as a means to alleviating their socio-economic problems (Coninck, 1992). Development initiative to these communities imply growth in the local economy, in the number of jobs created and undertakings that address aspirations of the community such as building a school. Socio-economic growth is viewed as an indication of strength and a matter of considerable community pride. Community development is thus viewed as a key to achieving set goals (Levy, 1981; Reinhard & Summers, 1981). In examining the process of community development, the challenge for communities has been how best to facilitate and manage the entire process of a chosen development strategy. Connected to this fact and when viewed in the context of a declining economic base, the task has been to stabilise the local economy in the short-term with the hope of a return to longer-term economic health (Bergman & Goldstein, 1983; Fullington, 1983). In most community organisations to date, the primary goal of development initiatives is the achievement of a viable economy and overall community well-being (Hunker, 1974; Tweeten & Brinkman, 1976). The achievement of this goal requires the integration of community-based economic development principles into actual practice.

Until recently, community development has been geared to attracting external investment, preferably a large manufacturing concern (Malizia, 1985). To achieve this goal, communities produced brochures about their unique locational advantages and invested in roads, water and sewer services – the basic infrastructure required by industry, (Tweeten & Brinkman, 1976). Towns and villages developed large industrial parks and expropriated land for anticipated local economic growth. This reliance on local potential advantages and existing supporting infrastructural services remained the mainstay of most communities' economic development efforts (Bergman, 1981).

While these communities' economic development efforts have been impressive, the results have been disappointing. The comparative advantage sought (and claimed) by each community has been neutralised as more communities acquired similar services and facilities. Local governments seeking economic development often provided generous tax concessions, effectively (and popularly) transferring the burden of property tax revenues to the residents instead of corporate taxpayers. This policy framework has had far-reaching implications, to the extent where anticipated local economic spin-offs to area business could not be assumed, as inputs to the production process were acquired on the basis of least cost and not community loyalty.

Ben-David Val (1980), Malizia (1985) and Peterson (1980) have discussed the typical economic development planning process. To these authors the process is similar to the familiar rational planning system used by regional planners and comprises steps beginning with data collection and ending with monitoring and evaluation of progress. As the plan evolves, the analysis should clearly support the choice of community economic development direction, objectives should be closely supportive of goals, the projects selected should demonstrate their contribution to community economic development targets, and on-going monitoring should facilitate continuous revisions to the plan as circumstances warrant (So, 1984).

The traditional goal of community development has been the enhancement of community well-being through improvements in public services and strengthening the local economy (Hunker, 1974; Tweeten & Brinkman, 1976; Malizia, 1985). In the process, the community and its continued viability then became the focus of local community development efforts (Davis et al, 1975). Over time, economic development planning remained community-based with the guidance of a trained practitioner who possessed skills required to carry out economic development in a competitive environment (Ben-David Val; 1980; Malizia, 1985). This then placed skills development and training as essential elements in community-based economic development initiatives.

In linking to the aforementioned discussion, it is acknowledged that while community development principles and processes are easily understood, many obstacles exist which diminish their potential applications in local community development. This is due to several factors. Many small communities resent planning of any kind because of the clash in priority between government and local community (Hodge & Qadeer, 1983). What is regarded by government as a priority may not necessarily be high on the local community's own agenda. In addition, small community administrators may lack the skills required to carry out economic development planning effectively and are often more comfortable with daily administrative tasks (Chow, 1981; Sokolow, 1982). In view of the complex socio-political and economic framework, community leaders are often unaware of the forces that directly contribute to the growth or decline of their community. Due to this complexity, most community investments are made without adequate understanding of community development process and corresponding impacts of related initiatives (Blakely & Bradshaw, 1982).

Local governments have very little discretion or autonomy in the management of their communities. This is because local government's mandate is determined by provincial legislative requirements and/or policies and programmes which unfortunately end up stalling and thwarting community decision-making (Plunkett & Betts, 1978; Higgins, 1977). This is compounded by a rising number of provincial and central (federal) agencies offering programme aid to communities, thereby posing problems of co-ordination and streamlining (Bergman, 1983). In this regard, extending training to local leaders fosters successful management of projects for their own communities (Bibi, 1990).

In view of the above mentioned constraints, the introduction of development initiatives to communities should take into account existing constraints and opportunities. Small communities and villages cannot afford major investments in staff resources to carry out local community development planning. Thus, the planning approach must make optimal use of existing local resources. By implication, it is more effective to train local administrators in local community development planning. This education and training should also be extended to local politicians who may be more familiar with the highly visible evidence of traditional or physical planning such as the development of land and services. The planning system as a process and a product must be accessible to the community at large, not limited to council, committees and staff only (Detomasi, 1984). In this process, an open method of decision-making and implementation assistance is necessary to garner community-wide support for local community development.

Conclusion

This section has examined the various forms community development initiatives take. It is important to point out the importance of interconnections between private, community, non-governmental and public sector organisations. These interconnections, however, influence the effective operation of each and every organisation in an environment of resource scarcity and increasing competition. Continued viability requires the presence of a factor or set of factors that provide an organisation with an advantage over its competitors. In the same way, communities interested in pursuing community development initiatives need to operate in a highly competitive environment (UNCRD, 1992). There are factors that contribute to the achievement of a competitive advantage in a community setting. The two most important are the availability of certain basic community services and community members' willingness to actively participate in the entire process of the development initiative. The community with an enhanced understanding of its potential and its position within an identifiable operating environment can generate a firm sense of direction to carry out appropriate and effective community development initiatives (Malizia, 1985).

The chapter has revealed that communities which rely on the more common ad hoc decision-making process experience missed opportunities and wasted public resources. This preliminary stage is crucial as it impacts the entire community development process. Furthermore, the community must understand the nature of its local economy, identify its strengths and weaknesses, and act to support its assets while minimising liabilities (Ben-David Val, 1980). Communities do not evolve independently of other economic systems, rather, they are part of the larger socio-economic framework. Walker (1980) stresses the need for communities to understand this relationship and to identify the linkages between the community and its wider environment. When adequately trained in the techniques of data collection and analysis, a community is then equipped to develop appropriate and viable community development strategies.

It is important to recognise that community development remains a sector within a socio-political and economic framework. Given the scarcity of resources for development initiatives, active community involvement in the decision-making process for their community direction becomes imperative. Despite this recognition, existing community development planning literature subordinates the external aspect of community economic development planning, although regional planners in their planning literature emphasise the need to carry out both steps (internal and external) in the community development planning process (So, 1984). While community development planning is similar to the rational planning models used by regional planners, (So, 1984) and those for programme planning in adult education (Beal et al., 1966; Boone, 1971; Boyle, 1981; Houle, 1972; Kidd, 1973; Knowles, 1970; Sork, 1994; Tyler, 1949), a major point of difference lies in strategic planning's emphasis on constant scanning of the community's internal and external environments in a conscious attempt to keep the organisation aware of its potential, to minimise the negative impacts of weaknesses or threats, thereby remain competitive and more importantly, viable.

This chapter has presented a literature review on the body of work which, in addition to espousing the notion of community development, advocates it as a potentially useful mechanism for the alleviation of the socio-economic problems of people below the poverty line. Furthermore, the chapter examined models for community development from which central ideas and expressions of community development were illuminated. Community development, therefore, expresses itself in several forms including; community development as a method, a process, an institutional initiative and a social movement. The chapter has also indicated that successful and effective community development initiatives share elements that enable a broad range of initiatives to fit under the umbrella term – community development. Notably these include local participation in decision-making and planning, focus on local initiative and leadership development through skills training and education, an emphasis on self-help and self-reliance, a belief in co-operation and collaboration within and outside of the community, the optimum utilisation of locally owned resources, consciousness-raising and empowerment of the people, and local community control over resources.

The chapter has noted that while community development principles and expressions are easily understood, several factors impede the effective implementation of development initiatives. These obstacles range from community resentment of planning due to negative experiences with public officials, deficient knowledge about community potential and opportunities, and lack of training in community development theories, techniques and practices. As part of its conclusion, the chapter emphasises the need to train and educate community members on community development practices and other techniques that ensure competitiveness amidst scarce resources from the public purse.

While training is a necessary component of the development process, communities are often confronted by socio-political forces that interfere with their efforts to achieve set goals. Communities then respond by seeking ways and means to achieving their aspirations irrespective of the government authority's level of involvement. In this book the DISSA development initiative is presented as a case for understanding the relationship between successive governments and the citizens who strive to improve their standard of living. DISSA was founded in 1986 in a country (Uganda) that has had eight[6] successive governments (civilian and military) since gaining political independence from Britain.

In addition to exploring the interface between community, politics and government, the next chapter aims to relate the theoretical premise and central ideas of community development to actual development initiative (DISSA). The main aim of the next chapter is to link established theory to practice and examine the practitioners' approach to the notion of community development as a field of study.

---

[6] After Uganda gained independence in 1962 the successive governments were: Obote I, 1962-1971; Idi Amin, 1971- 1979; Yusuf Lule, 1979; Godfrey Binaisa, 1979; The Military Commission, 1979-1980; Obote II, 1980-85, Tito Okello, 1985-86 and Yoweri Museveni, 1986-to date.

Chapter III
Community Development in Practice

This chapter describes DISSA (Displaced Students Association), an adult youth development initiative, in north-western Uganda (Figure 3). In order to better understand the immediate problems that led to the establishment of DISSA, an overview of the political history of Uganda shall precede a description of the development initiative.

Uganda: An Historical Overview

The Republic of Uganda, a land-locked country in East Africa, is situated on the equator (Figure 1). The name Uganda is a Kiswahili term for the entire country comprising the four former kingdoms of Buganda, Bunyoro, Ankole and Toro on the one hand, and on the other, the regions of Lango, Acholi, Madi, West Nile, Bukedi, Bugisu, Busoga, Teso, Karamoja, Sebei and Kigezi which were added to the protectorate during the period of British colonial rule. Uganda is bounded by Sudan in the north, Kenya in the east, Tanzania and Rwanda in the south, and Zaire in the west. It covers a geographic area of 94,000 sq. miles (236,580 sq. km), (Ibingira, 1973; Sathyamurthy, 1986; Omara-Otunnu, 1987). The country owes much of its strategic importance as the source of the River Nile that flows through Sudan, Ethiopia, Egypt and into the Mediterranean Sea. The 1993 Population Census recorded 18 million people in Uganda[7]. There are fifteen major ethnic groups that fit under four main language clusters namely, Bantu, Luo, Nilo-Hamitic and Sudanic. Broadly speaking, the Bantu-speakers are to be found in the south and west of the country, Luo in the north, Nilo-Hamitic in the south and Sudanic in the north-west.

---

[7] Bartholomew's (1995).

The tragedy is that at the time of political independence in 1962 Uganda's relative standing was far higher. In the 1960s, it was viewed as one of the most promising economies of sub-Sahara Africa. From 1963 to 1970, economic growth averaged 6% a year and Uganda had the fourth highest GDP per capita in the whole sub-Sahara region (Sathyamurthy, 1986; de Coninck, 1992). After Idi Amin's overthrow of the Milton Obote I government on January 25, 1971, the country was immediately racked by political and economic turmoil, a succession of internal strife and mass killings which had a prolonged and devastating effect on the economic, social and civil life of the country (Omara-Otunnu, 1987).

At the start of the 1970s, major parts of the modern sectors of the economy were in the hands of the Asian community. Idi Amin's expulsion of some 80,000 Asians (initially a popularly acclaimed move), transformed both the economic and cultural fabric of major areas of Uganda's society, with far-reaching implications to the present day. This included the abandonment and closing down of a wide range of productive enterprises and political confusion over the ownership of both commercial and residential properties (Sathyamurthy, 1986; Omara-Otunnu, 1987; de Coninck, 1992). Most of these properties were 'given' by Idi Amin to his henchmen.

After the 'Liberation War' and Idi Amin's overthrow, Uganda attempted to reconstruct its shattered economy. Like his predecessor Yusuf Lule, on May 13, 1980, the Military Commission accused President Binaisa's administration of corruption and consequently assumed the powers of the Presidency (Sathyamurthy, 1986; Omara-Otunnu, 1987). With some order restored after Binaisa's departure, the Military Commission announced a general election set for December 1980. After a period of initial optimism, however, the Obote II regime ushered in a period of further violence and destruction. This was accelerated by the rival claimants[8] to political power who had been disappointed by the 1980 election results that was allegedly rigged (Omara-Otunnu, 1987). The chaotic and anarchic behaviour of the national army and challenge of the guerrilla forces

---

[8] This included, first, the National Resistance Movement (NRM) led by Yoweri Museveni, and its fighting force, the National Resistance Army (NRA); secondly, the Former Uganda National Army (FUNA); third, the Uganda National Rescue Front (UNRF); fourth Uganda Freedom Movement (UFM) and fifth the Federal Democratic Movement of Uganda (FEDEMU) (Omara-Otunnu, 1987: p. 157).

(the National Resistance Army led by Yoweri Museveni) further weakened Obote II's effective grip on power.

On July 27, 1985 a substantial faction of the Army led by Brigadier Bajilio Olara Okello (fearing victimisation by a faction led by Brigadier Smith Opon Achak), marched from the north to Uganda's capital Kampala and seized power. Proclaimed as Head of State and Chairman of the Military Council, General Tito Okello pursued a peaceful process with the warring parties and succeeded in the signing of the Nairobi Peace Accord in 1985. The inadequacy of the Military Council (evident in its lack of action plan) and the intransigence of the NRM/NRA prevented the accord from ever being implemented.

On January 25, 1986 the military fights culminated in the overthrow of the Military Council and seizure of power by the NRM/NRA. Since then, Yoweri Museveni has remained the President of Uganda. It is Museveni's government that created a conducive political climate to local organisations and initiatives such as DISSA.

DISSA Community Development Initiative

HISTORICAL BACKGROUND AND TRADITIONS

Uganda[9] prides itself as the source of the River Nile and is commonly referred to as the "Pearl of Africa"[10] because of its lush tropical forests, its cultural diversity, and rich natural resources[11]. Prior to foreign contact, the political structure of Uganda took the form of what was termed interlacustrine[12] kingdoms, a significant factor that united the people for a period of time against foreign aggression (Sathyamurthy, 1986; Twaddle, 1993).

---

[9] Uganda has a population of around 18.8 million. In 1989, its gross domestic product (GDP) was estimated to be $4.46 billion, giving a GDP per capita of $272 in that year. With such a low level of per capita income, Uganda is classified as one of the 42 least developed counties': according to World Bank data, it is the 22nd poorest country in the world – and the 13th poorest in Africa – in terms of GNP per capita (World Bank: 1989a, p.64).

[10] A name given by Sir Winston L. Churchill in his book *My African Journey*, 1908.

[11] This includes minerals, wildlife, fertile soils and headwaters of the great Nile River.

[12] Interlacustrine refers to "within the Lake Victoria basin".

POLITICAL

The Nilotic peoples of Uganda that comprise the Alur, Lango, Badama, Jonam and Acholi, were a product of the Luo migration from southern Sudan (Table I). Community governance was often controlled by kings, and at the grass roots by chiefs for a particular kingdom. Prominent kingdoms that existed were Bunyoro-Kitara, Buganda, Toro and Ankole (Southall, 1953; Sathyamurthy, 1986; Twaddle, 1993). The Nebbi community formed part of the Alur dynasty with clan chiefs called *Rwodhi*[13]. Each Rwoth was regarded as the trustee-owner of the land attached to his clan. The authority of the Rwodhi was by no means considerable (Southall, 1953). A major responsibility of the Rwodhi was the collection and storage of tributes from the various clans every crop harvest season. This would then be utilised as collective security in times of crises such as floods and droughts. The Rwoth controlled the community's resources and mobilised the people in times of foreign aggression. During disputes, elders would be summoned to a hearing and reconciliation of conflicts between plaintiffs and punishments were enforced in the form of manual (hard) labour and fines in form of livestock (Southall, 1953).

ECONOMIC

Up until the 1890s, barter trade was the major form of exchange, and the most precious commodity was iron bars used for the manufacture of hoes, machetes and axes. Hunting and gathering, livestock raising and crop cultivation were the most common forms of production (Southall, 1953).

The Anglo-German Agreement of 1890 brought Uganda under the British sphere of influence. A trading company – the Imperial British East Africa Company (IBEA) – was given a Royal Charter to trade with and administer Uganda. Three years later, by the Uganda Agreement of 1893, Britain took full control of the country's administration and declared it a "protectorate" (Mamdani, 1983). For the Alur, the transition to commercial agriculture and other tasks that required a substantive labour force were achieved by communal labour

---

[13] Rwodhi is the plural of Rwoth. (See Southall, 1953).

– *Koya*[14] under the direction of the community mobiliser, referred to as Nyampara, an arrangement that was later adopted in the 19th Century by the British system of indirect rule (Sathyamurthy, 1986).

SOCIAL

Social status was attributed to Age, (elders having more status than younger members of the village), Gender (males had higher status than females), Marriage (a polygamist gained most authority and this included traditional Rwoth who were mostly polygamous), and Occupation (i.e., a skilled poacher and warrior had high standing). Social harmony and bondship was fostered through festive seasons, rituals, and gatherings at local beer clubs. This reinforced social relationships between persons in the community.

Bride-price, which the groom's family was obligated to pay to the bride's father in the form of livestock, resulted in marriage whereby the bride would leave her family and go to live with her husband's family. This has continued to the present day Alur society (Southall, 1953).

The Alur tribe, a subset of the Luo, have a common traditional understanding with other Luo tribes across the three countries of southern Sudan, northern Uganda, and north-western Kenya. However, there are many different localised dialects (i.e., the original Alur, Acholi, Langi, Jonam, and the Badama).

RITUAL

Prior to the import of theism, spiritual practices were classed as animistic. Worshipping the spirit of the dead, in the form of shrines, large trees, mountains and streams, and offerings on such occasions of blood and organs of livestock, were meant to appease and create a union with the living. The witch-doctors were sought for healing and solving problems such as infertility, those possessed by evil spirits, and for the acquisition of wealth (Southall, 1953).

---

[14] Koya – a native term that refers to a collective action by the community in solving problems e.g., crop cultivation, bridge construction, shelter for the elderly and disadvantaged (DISSA Survey, 1995).

Project Background

COMMUNITY DEVELOPMENT PROCESS AND STRATEGY

The Nebbi community, covering a geographic area of 2,900 sq. km., comprises the three counties of Okoro, Padyere, and Jonam. It has a population of over 123,378 engaged primarily in three distinct economic activities, namely, the Jonam who live along the River Nile and are fishers, the Padyere who are both pastoralists and agriculturists and produce cash crops – cotton and cassava – and the Okoro who cultivate plantations of coffee, sugar-cane, banana, groundnuts, maize, and broad beans (Nebbi District Development Committee, 1990).

The root cause of the community problem was heavily felt after the Liberation War of 1979 that ousted the military government of Idi Amin Dada. DISSA (Displaced Students Association) was established when most students[15] could not further their education as a result of severe breakdown in the existing socio-political and economic infrastructure. Most prominent parents fled into neighbouring Zaire and Sudan and left their families behind. The departure of the breadwinners in families meant tuition and scholastic supplies could not be afforded despite the opening of schools after the end of the war. Owing to this dilemma, the youths' collective action was directed to a search for a solution to the crisis. Creation of alternative structures to address community socio-economic needs then became imperative. This was reinforced when the group recognised the low income generation in the rural sector despite abundant natural resources, and the lack of training in relevant skills for the economically productive age-bracket in their community.

More important was the need to put an end to the environmental degradation which resulted from the application of traditional farming techniques in the community. This required the promotion of community awareness of the lingering environmental hazard. The new government of Museveni had pledged a commitment to creating an independent, self-sustaining and integrated national economy. Local development initiatives were highly supported by the new government. DISSA believed that the availability and enhancement of

---

[15] DISSA Adult/Youth comprises college level students between the ages 18 and 30 years.

local resources was a springboard to achieving their goals of local community development.

DISSA considered the establishment of a marketing channel for local produce (simsim, groundnuts, maize, coffee and cotton) to urban areas as a possibility to revitalise cash flow in the community. Furthermore, forest availability in the Lendu forest (the planning zone of Awang and Ossi in Okoro county), that the government allowed for timber harvesting, was an attractive alternative activity.

Scraps of vehicles damaged during the 1979 liberation war exposed an avenue for potential raw material in the production of tools and other implements by local blacksmiths. Moreover, DISSA identified the need for improved transportation. This would bring a dual benefit: first, the generation of revenues for the programme and second, in meeting the high demand for essential products from Kampala where most manufacturing and processing industries are based (400 km. from Nebbi town).

GETTING STARTED

With the influential community philosophy of self-help, DISSA mobilised community participation by way of financial and material contributions towards the project. Full participation by all members (e.g., the management responsibility of the organisation rotated amongst members) facilitated the establishment of the programmes. People were encouraged to know as many activities of the organisation as possible to expedite the smooth operation of their projects. In 1986 five original members registered DISSA with the Ministry of Women in Development, Culture and Youth. Registration with a statutory body gave the group legitimate recognition and support in dissemination of their action programme to the community. Through member contributions, the group embarked on a small-scale income-generating activity – crop production. The group later expanded to retailing essential commodities, especially sundry items (i.e., salt, cooking oil, soap, and paraffin); and to ensure its commercial viability, it embarked on marketing maize, beans, simsim, cassava flour, groundnuts, and fish to external markets. In 1988, DISSA started pit-sawing and tree harvesting activities under the guidance of the forestry extension workers. The forestry extension services were part of the government's emergency forestry rehabilitation programme. With the production of timber, the group was in a position to begin carpentry and joinery, specialising in meeting the needs of the local people resettling after the end of the liberation war (e.g., simple furniture, door and window-frames).

In view of the aforementioned problems, DISSA established a community-initiative, a direct appeal of the Museveni government's efforts in the task of rural development, self-employment, rehabilitation and nation building (Museveni, 1985). Second, the group sought to engage the community in village-appropriate skills, training in carpentry and joinery, blacksmithing, bricklaying and other handicrafts. The third objective was to undertake, demonstrate, and encourage improved methods of agro-forestry.

An equally overriding priority for DISSA was the need to expand the group's existing activities to a level which ensured the generation of adequate income to achieve self-sustainable yield in all sub-units. Furthermore, DISSA aimed to evolve a strategy of building the organisation's capacity, by first embarking on those activities that would ensure fast production of surplus funds, thereby enabling them to address other needs of the Nebbi community.

A long-term goal of the group (after three years, 1995-1998) is to engage in metal fabrication, to enlarge the transport network, to construct an orphanage centre, and to be well-established financially through accumulation of protective capital (PAM, 1992).

Project Organisation and Activities

DISSA employs a team method of administration, with an executive committee of five members, consisting of chairperson or director (formerly called co-ordinator), secretary, financial controller, manager, supervisor, and four members at large. The project units are managed by four departmental managers, as portrayed in the management flow chart (Figure 4).

FORESTRY

Projects in the field of reforestation, thinning, and harvesting have been ongoing since the unit was created. With small-scale lumber activity in the forest planning zone[16] (3,373 hectares with tree planting and lumbering activities having begun in 1940 in Okoro county, about 60 km. to the north of Nebbi town), the sawmill cuts up to one truck load (6 cu. metres) of wood per day in the form of sawn lumber and timber planks. This has a total market value of US$180, daily providing enough income to cover expenses of operation, maintenance, repairs, and replacement. Besides the softwood lumber production, the group manually operates a 2.5 metre pit-saw on scattered woodlots of mahogany throughout the district although the government limits the cutting of hardwood. A Kara sawmill, and a 76-78 HP tractor with trailer are located at the site in Lendu forest. The group has also been involved in community reforestation.

TRANSPORTATION

The newly procured seven ton truck delivers to the community durable consumer goods and essential products. In addition the transportation and delivery of sold furniture for domestic and office uses, timber planks, cured bricks for construction purposes are ensured through the availability of the truck. The truck hauling service has generated a positive cash flow that has enabled the opening of a savings account at the Uganda Commercial Bank – Nebbi branch, that would in the long run take charge of replacing the truck, buying additional construction materials, and boosting capital accumulation. The group has six bicycles which are used to identify farmers in need of marketing their produce and crops, after which the truck hauling operation is made to pick up, transfer and deliver to buyers. DISSA has become a significant indigenous buyer and exporter (from the region) of locally grown crops such as maize, beans, cotton, simsim, groundnuts, and tobacco. Hauling this produce as far as Kampala has increased their present sales activity tenfold. The distribution of tree seedlings for DISSA's community tree planting activity has continued to be accomplished at minimum cost because of the community ownership of the truck.

---

[16] The Lendu forest planning zone covers 3,373 hectares with tree planting and lumbering activities having begun in 1940. Today this plantation contains mature softwood trees such as cypress and pines (DISSA Survey, 1995).

In order to enhance their skills in product management and the application of appropriate village-level technology, fifty additional youths have been trained to achieve the target of meeting increased demand for local implements (machetes, hoes, charcoal stoves, hammers, axes, plane blades, vice and chisels), and tourist related items (arrows, knives, and spears blades). The fifty participants upon graduation embarked on carpentry and blacksmithing instruction in the community, and more specifically at the Pakwach Tools Production and Training Centre (23 km. south of DISSA's main site) (PAM, 1992). Another training programme covered inventory stock handling and control, which has assisted the sales unit in expanding to its present two outlets in Nebbi and Paila. The retail store operation has made DISSA a significant supplier to Nebbi and the neighbouring communities of essential commodity supplies. More recently, DANIDA[17] has worked with members of DISSA, assisting in the assessment and implementation of their training needs. Staff training and retraining has continued in the various sections of accounting and bookkeeping, carpentry and joinery, truck driving and maintenance and inventory control.

WORKSHOP CONSTRUCTION

The construction of a larger woodworking shop (8 x 25 metres) commenced in 1995 and involved using the truck for transportation of sand and stones gathered by community volunteers as part of a community contribution in absorbing higher overhead costs. Hence, available funds meet the actual cost of fuel and driver.

Implementation

THE PROCESS

At present DISSA has a store in Nebbi and another in Paila, about 30 km. south of Nebbi, towards Pakwach, on the shores of the River Nile. Because their base supplies are intermittent, there is difficulty in maintaining a regular supply of fish stocks on hand. However,

---

[17] DANIDA acronym for Danish International Development Agency, currently engaged in rehabilitation and reconstruction of the dilapidated socio-economic infrastructure in Uganda since 1986 (DISSA Survey, 1995).

during March 1994, DISSA reported their largest stock in sundry items valued at US$1,500 and that it was sold in a fortnight. The largest amount of grain that they had to purchase for any sale at any one time was one ton which was sold in Kampala. This is about one seventh the amount they could handle with their own truck, if given the funds to purchase the available stocks held by farmers.

The DISSA group co-ordinator, Garbet Alichan, learned of the African Development Foundation (ADF) from an old copy of the Kenyan newspaper – *The Daily Nation* (published on August 30, 1985), which he found in a Kampala public library in 1989. During 1991 Alichan met with a representative from the ADF to discuss DISSA's programme proposal in the hope of obtaining funding. The ADF responded favourably and arrangements were made to visit the project site. The group's unit leaders and members had a chance to ask questions with respect to their various departments. For example, carpentry issues were handled by those individuals involved in carpentry training and practice and sales issues were handled by those individuals involved in essential commodity sales. In their assessment criteria, the ADF was convinced the Association could be a 'vehicle' for achieving community rehabilitation and development. They were impressed by DISSA's demonstrated resourcefulness, dedication and their capacity for working productively as a group under difficult circumstances. Furthermore, DISSA's involvement in income-generating activities that were sensitive to the surrounding physical and human environment, indicated their integrated approach to resource development and management.

Their endeavour to expand the scale of production entailed letters to the Ministry of Women in Development, Culture and Youth, the Town Clerk and the Nebbi District Development Committee. At a secondary level, documentation from the Commissioner of Lands and Water Resources gave the group access to the land for an initial period of five years extendible to forty-nine years. In addition, an official site plan for the 15.62 hectares of land was obtained from the Ministry of Housing and Urban Development. At the present moment, the Land title is being processed alongside the document supported by the following programme instruments: project work plan, training curriculum for carpentry and blacksmithing, DISSA by-laws, a detailed current financial-year report, and a documentary letter of intent from the Pakwach Tools Production and Training Centre to train selected members from their community. Total expenses of action plan implemented was estimated at US$186,844.

The DISSA blacksmith shop produces tools and implements, using appropriate forms of technology, which are of good quality, at affordable prices for people in the community. This has tremendously helped the community save precious foreign exchange which is better utilised in procuring items that are not easily substituted within the local economy.

During the implementation process, outside expertise was called upon to aid the group in making technical decisions, such as the operation of machinery, creating standards for sustainable yield and organisation and methods. The group decisions were supported by government policy aimed at promoting local development initiatives. Seasonal changes influenced decisions pertaining to group programmes and activities to be carried out in any given period.

However, at times the project faced stiff resistance from groups that represent other interests in the community. A case in point was the struggle over land tenure between DISSA and elder groups as the latter interpreted the process as another encroachment on their long-held land rights.

CHRONOLOGY OF PROJECT IMPLEMENTATION

Although the implementation plan was very broad, the DISSA project undertaking commenced in October, 1992.

Year One

MONTHS 1-6

The project management team was established. The offices of all department heads were set up and became functional through field supervision. In view of the members' recommendations, the project co-ordinator, with the work supervisors drew up a detailed implementation plan for all project activities. Funds were disbursed for the procurement of primary items (i.e., office supplies, initial supply of essential commodities) to be sold at DISSA store outlets, bookkeeping materials, training in truck and machine maintenance, and management and organisational development[18]. This phase was

---

[18] The ADF Project Appraisal Memorandum (1992: p. 4).

concluded by clearing the land and collecting locally available materials such as stones and sand, for later transportation to the workshop construction site.

MONTHS 7-12

The second phase featured training of the members at the Pakwach Tools Production Centre, continued construction of a carpentry workshop, and ordering and procurement of pitsaws, hand tools, bicycles, tractor and trailer. The programme concentrated on timber production and horticulture as major activities. Outreach activities to surrounding farmers (to inform them of the availability of transport for their produce to the market) were a prominent function of the project. Their stores were stocked with assorted items that made it a significant supplier of essential commodities in the Nebbi community. A concluding activity of this phase was the establishment of an active savings account with the Uganda Commercial Bank, Nebbi branch.

Year Two

MONTHS 1-6

The workshop construction was completed and blacksmith plus carpentry activities commenced. For the first 3-6 months, four instructors (two at a time) from the Pakwach Tools Production Centre worked with DISSA's trained members to assist in teaching their newly acquired skills to their members. This was followed by the continued expansion of year one activities.

MONTHS 7-12

DISSA hoped to establish its own training programme and recruit new members and trainees. In addition all other activities continued as scheduled.

Year Three

In the final year of ADF funding for the project, DISSA planned to evaluate its progress and identify which income-generating activities had been most promising. This process would enable the project to realistically assess prioritisation of fund disbursement for future activities. They will also look into the quality of their operation and further strengthen their community building activities accordingly.

Linkages

COMMUNITY-BASED GROUPS

The philosophy DISSA applied in building the project was emulated and later led to the formation of other youth groups in the community. For example, the Nebbi Adungu Young Group organised a small-scale savings and business enterprise and the Nebbi Muslim Youth Society has built a primary school and is in the process of establishing a community-based health care centre.

NON-GOVERNMENTAL ORGANISATION

The Euro-action ACORD (European Agency Consortium for Research and Development) and World Vision International conducted a training needs assessment for DISSA. DANIDA contributed toward training in management, financial control, stock management, and project start-up. The ADF signed an agreement for a three-year grant on July 24, 1992 that formalised plans for project expansion (i.e., procurement of tractors, truck, Kara sawmill). A financial management specialist was assigned to work with the group in the early stages of the project to set up financial accounting systems through continued meetings with DISSA members.

GOVERNMENT

The Government of Uganda supported DISSA through the signing of an agreement with the ADF, enabling the project expansion to take place. The ADF ministry contact (finance and planning) ensured that any imported commodities and equipment for DISSA would arrive duty-free.

SECTORAL

Many farmers now sell agricultural produce to DISSA's silos, which is later transported via their truck to towns and urban centres as far away as Kampala, enabling local farmers to expand their markets.

Most DISSA members are displaced students from the 1979 Liberation War who lost hope of completing their education. This programme helped direct the youths aspirations to constructive channels as they obtained gainful employment and participated in decisions pertaining to community resource use. The displaced students and others have reasonable levels of academic qualifications ('O' level Cambridge Certificate Level) which has facilitated effective management of project sub-units.

The project has promoted community consciousness in the preservation and protection of a sustainable and healthy environment. Group meetings have resulted in enlightening residents on current health-related issues (e.g., immunisation against the six killer diseases[19]).

DISSA, via its truck transport system, plays the part of courier, handling and submitting documents (e.g., retirement application forms, land title papers, pension forms, insurance, trade licenses) between the residents in Nebbi and government ministries and private organisations in Kampala.

Impact Assessment

PRIMARY AND SECONDARY BENEFITS

The training of community members on site at minimum cost will directly benefit seventy-six members from both DISSA and neighbouring communities. The provision of essential commodities and furniture (especially door and window-frames), assists residents in the community with respect to improved communication, transportation, and timely delivery of products. Secondary beneficiaries – the cash crop and vegetable farmers benefit from reduced hauling rates and transport-related problems in marketing their produce. This has reduced handling and spoilage of produce. In addition, DISSA's truck transport has provided the community with a number of spin-offs in the form of increased goods and services, better access to markets and the movement of building materials from industrial towns in southern Uganda that are not readily available in Nebbi. Moreover, the transportation of tree seedlings to promote DISSA's community tree planting activity through individual households has benefited the entire community, and more readily,

---

[19] This includes smallpox, measles, polio, cholera, chicken-pox and tetanus (de Coninck, 1992).

helped the soil erosion prevention (including serving as windbreaks) and providing construction poles.

DISSA members benefit from the provision of medical treatment allowances, including their extended families. Another advantage extended to members is the availability of personal loans and advances without collateral[20]. The general meeting reviews from time-to-time the maximum that may be loaned or advanced to any individual DISSA member. The loans are however first approved by the committee.

COMMUNITY PARTICIPATION

The group is working with the community to educate them on the value of agro-forestry. The 15.62 hectares of land was set up and designed with a portion for demonstration farming systems. Through this approach, improved agriculture and forest activities can be observed and studied by the local community.

The net gain resulting from these operations is apportioned, based on consensus, at DISSA's annual general meetings. Many members are not paid a full salary. The group fixes the acceptable liability which the organisation may incur through loans from other institutions, as well as fixing the sum which may be loaned to any member.

The DISSA members plan activities based on informal discussions with community members, through social gatherings such as annual cultural festivals, social clubs, and women's groups. This enables DISSA to ensure that their plans coincide with the needs of the community. Income is divided as specified in their by-law (i.e., 25% for reserve fund, 30% for investment, 30% for operating expenses, and 15% distributed equally amongst members).

TECHNICAL

The Indian-made five-ton truck (Tata) is widely used in Uganda, and is considered quite reliable, with spare parts locally made in Kampala auto-centres at reasonable cost when compared with (genuine parts of) European-made trucks. The portable Kara circular sawmill is more appropriate for softwoods and saws with less waste compared to other alternative mills. More importantly, it can be operated by a

---

[20] DISSA by-laws p.3.

tractor through the power take off (PTO) unit which is more suitable in the remote areas where DISSA operates.

GOVERNMENT POLICY

The Kara sawmill meets the government of Uganda's desire to achieve an accelerated rehabilitation programme, through minimum human and capital resource outlays. Since it is specifically adapted to use with softwood species it is in line with the government's strategy to reduce harvesting of hardwoods[21] in order to preserve the tropical forests. The government is currently operating the same mills in other locations and is managing a central training unit in the operation, maintenance, and repairs.   There is no tuition fee, save for accommodation, scholastic materials and meals. More importantly, parts for this unit have been made available duty free in order to reduce their cost and hence increase the economic viability of sawmill operations.   The government's Ministry of Forestry in conjunction with the Norwegian Forestry Agency, provides technical assistance in the area of nursery management and sustainable yield harvesting of softwood timber supplies.

SOCIAL/CULTURAL

The project has encouraged DISSA members to practice a spirit of thrift, mutual self-help, and improved education.   Community participation that reflects Ugandan social and communal traditions of working in a group is realised through sharing of the group's proceeds and profits with community groups (e.g., sponsoring medi-care, clothing and education for orphans). The co-existence of appropriate forms of technology and modern methods has ensured continued preservation of local culture and social values. Social identity of the group with the community is enhanced through participation of their football club in local district tournaments and has the full moral and material support of the community.

Most of the members are well-educated and are now working in the project sub-units instead of emigrating to industrial towns, which has reduced 'brain drain' from the local area. Three out of thirty-two members have parents working in the civil service and the remainder

---

[21] Mahogany is the dominant species in this location, often growing to a circumference of six metres and to a height of fifty metres.

are daughters and sons of peasant farmers. Commodities and social services brought nearer to the Nebbi community via better transport and capital accumulation from these activities is expended mostly in Nebbi, thus reducing leakage from the local economy.

POLITICAL

All levels of government – central, regional, district and local – recognise DISSA as a legal entity. This is reinforced by the National Resistance Movement (N.R.M.) government's ten-point programme, in which the tenth point spells out "building an independent, self-sustaining and integrated national economy"[22]. The government recognised DISSA and consequently approved a grant through ADF to the tune of US$186,844 to help achieve that target at the micro-level.

ENVIRONMENT

The major impact of this project has been in the area of forestry. The Government of Uganda puts much emphasis on reforestation and conservation, and has attracted many external donors working in this field. At the local level, the group has been working with District forestry officials to implement the stringent "one tree planted for each one harvested" programme, which is part of the government's environmental policy to mitigate the desertification encroachment south of the Sahara desert. Use of the sawmill has reduced damage to nearby vegetation, as it ensures sawing operation of logs on site, thus eliminating the need to drag or haul entire trees through the forest. With the added equipment (tractor and truck) the group has been able to assist and improve the main trail in the forest limiting soil erosion which tends to occur otherwise. The Nebbi District Forestry Department provides all the technical assistance necessary in establishing nurseries, thereby strengthening replacement of the trees harvested. This measure has made possible the local procurement of the cypress and pine seeds that were originally imported.

---

[22] The Ten Point Programme of the National Resistance Movement set the following programme priorities at the beginning of its administration; they include restoration and addressing i) democratic governance, ii) increased security, iii) fostering national unity, iv) promoting national independence, v) effective management of the national economy, vi) strengthening social services, vii) redressing misuse of power and public office, viii) redressing errors, ix) defending human and democratic rights and x) developing a mixed national economy (Museveni, 1985).

ECONOMIC

DISSA has developed experience in its activities and has income-expenditure calculations for every sub-unit. This indicates a clear understanding by the group of the distinction between income-generating and income-decreasing activities. For example, income-expenditure calculations (all figures in US funds) for truck operation (a trip from Nebbi to Kampala), with an average load of commodity (simsim) valued at $1,540 buying price and associated cost (fuel $124, driver allowances of $50, loading charges $30, security parking $30, spare parts $73 general service $21, insurance $9, license $2, miscellaneous $20, and depreciation $156), generates a surplus of $955. On the return from Kampala to Nebbi, the truck is loaded with essential commodities worth $4,950, fuel $124, driver allowance $50, tyre $150, loading $30, security packing $30, spare parts $73, service $21, insurance $9, license $2, miscellaneous $20, and depreciation $156; for a total cost of $5605. This generates a net profit of $610, less costs of supplies and delivery. Thus a single return trip total income is $9,450, less total costs of $7,800 for a net profit of $1,650. In a conservative three months the group realised a profit of $9,000 (two trips per month multiplied by three months) to cover the costs of purchasing future supplies ($6,490) for resale plus one half the same amount to be in stock at stores at any given time. After the third month the profits generated covered their recurrent costs and this enabled essential commodity trade to be self-sustaining.

The log sawing machine is an activity that is flexible in that it has a 'fall-back'[23] (secondary) income-generating use, should conditions temporarily change (e.g., if the demand for local truck hauling decreases). DISSA makes more trips to Kampala with crop produce. The carpentry section alternates between manufacturing value-added office furniture or more locally-demanded chairs (johnie sets), tables, windows, and door frames should market conditions change. This multi-use flexibility within all project components ensures that a solid economic base is always possible.

---

[23] 'Fall-back' in this context implies flexibility in shifts of production depending on the prevailing forces of demand.

RESOURCE MANAGEMENT AND DEVELOPMENT

The project ensures resource renewal and over all sustainable yield criteria are met, with the on-going tree harvest and planting in the Lendu Forest Planning Zone. Besides planting trees in the forest, DISSA has its own nursery beds of five hundred seedlings for use by the larger community. In addition, this contributes to soil fertility enhancing crop and vegetable production. According to project executors, "some of the conservation practices planned and implemented in isolated regions are boundary cropping, alley cropping, living fences, windbreak, and shelter belts, inter cropping, compound planting and crop rotation"[24]. Besides farming methods, ornamental tree planning around individual homes is a common practice in Nebbi. The emphasis on village-appropriate technology minimises waste during the production process (i.e., using sawdust and shavings from sawmill for fuel in charcoal stoves), and enables full use of resources.

Impediments

The DISSA group has faced a number of constraints in working to realise their goals. First, the organisation had members, 40% of whom were unskilled in relation to the various project tasks and this posed a training challenge, blocking full participation in the project. Second, traditional chiefs in the area were sceptical about the group's motives and did not allow DISSA members easy access to land leased from the government. This group tried to discourage DISSA members from developing the land. However, this is a common occurrence because the traditional elders are conservative in customary practices and never appreciate outright development proposed in the locality. In addition, the traditional history of the Alur land ownership permits land purchase, whether for community work or not. Third, due to cultural constraints (a woman has to be highly educated to gain community authority and take part in effective decision-making processes), the womenfolk have found it challenging to participate fully in DISSA's programmes. Hence there are only three women who are active out of the total twenty-six core members in DISSA. Finally, DISSA's by-law under the Ugandan

---

[24] ADF Project Appraisal Memorandum, (1992: p.12).

Not-for-Profit Society Act, has limited outside participation by restricting membership to their original target group (i.e., displaced students association members) and this has thwarted comprehensive, full community involvement in decision-making.

Analysis

In the following analysis the author presents (based on community development literature of the central ideas and principles) a perceived notion of ideal characteristics for development initiatives against what was obtained (as contained in the questionnaire survey and the Appraisal Memo) at DISSA project. The ideal characteristics are in the normal font and DISSA initiatives in italics.

CULTURAL CONTINUITY

Cultural continuity is fostered in community development through an emphasis on community celebrations, holidays, and other activities that create a strong sense of belonging. This ensures that cultural ethics and values are imparted across generations, thus mitigating the threat posed by modernity which tends to fragment and segment society. Furthermore, handicraft and artisan production methods that depict many facets of community institutions are important cornerstones in perpetuating cultural practices and integrity. By building social cohesion within communities, there are often fewer problems with alienation, anomie and isolation, hence less need for national programmes that specifically target social problems which arise from community disintegration, thus freeing up resources to be used either in more beneficial pro-active ways, or ideally to reduce government borrowing.

The creation of an organisation by drawing membership from within the community and backed by the philosophy of communal self-help (Nyampara and Koya) that existed well before Ugandan contacts with foreign interests has helped social cohesion in DISSA to the present moment. Despite the breakdown in political and economic infrastructure, DISSA continued operating since the mobilisation techniques applied had a cultural attachment. The founding members who agreed on non-payment of their labour effort is a clear influence of culture on the project.

Furthermore, culture has impacted items the blacksmiths produce as it accommodates the traditional economic way of life, i.e. fish-hooks, arrow-heads, knife blades, hoes, machetes and axe heads.

DECISION-MAKING PROCESS

Community development is achieved through a broad-based community participation in the planning, decision-making, and implementation process. This level of participation fosters community identity and pride with the development initiative. The interests of all members, including women, youth, the elderly, the disabled, and minority groups are reflected in all aspects of community actions. Everyone is made to feel that their participation in decision-making is vital to the success of the programme. Every encouragement is extended to citizens' participation in planning, decision-making, and goal setting through channels which include forums and councils. These forums and councils undertake the role of resolving conflicts and fostering of practices that allow healing to take place between former adversaries.

It is difficult to determine from the information available whether or not DISSA involves the community in its decision-making process. Yet, it appears that an informal process of discussion with other community members allows for some feedback that may influence the decisions arrived at in their group planning sessions and general meetings. However it is not clear if consensus is used within the group other than in the smaller sub-units.

CONSCIOUSNESS-RAISING

The strength of a community development process is its focus on local initiatives, cultural practices, the reduction of harmful influences in the form of 'imported' culture and indoctrination (i.e., television, radio and film) in favour of local and culturally relevant 'live' performances. In the development process, the establishment of a clear step-by-step approach which allows the community to envision its long-term goals and objectives is important. In addition, a community education programme that sensitises citizens to the possibilities which lie dormant in other forms of organising political, social, cultural and economic relations is essential. Consciousness-raising facilitates community development as it ensures that every activity, whether implicit or explicit, is understood in its socio-cultural, economic and political context and that no action is isolated from other facets of the community.

The determination of DISSA members to develop successful enterprises within their own community, rather than drifting to urban centres to seek jobs, is an indication of a commitment of the group in bringing appropriate forms of development to Nebbi. By using their academic qualifications in this way they have acted as strong role models for other youth in the region, in deterring urban migration among the young. Development is a process that can be achieved over time and involves shifts in human perception with regards to depletion, restoration, conservation and good management techniques. An overriding concern in this process is the manner in which a community applies these concepts to the development initiative. It must be pointed out that DISSA has attempted to inculcate an awareness in its members and in the community at large of the need to harness resources in an efficient and sustainable manner.

COMMUNITY PARTICIPATION

Community participation facilitates development initiatives as it emphasises more voluntary community work and the sharing of benefits that result from the collective efforts. It also helps ensure community members have a more active involvement in citizenship duties. In the participatory process, members of the community understand that their involvement needs to be an active one rather than mere "passengers on the development bus". Community participation create avenues for a continually revolving information network within community members and the maintenance of adequate feedback for the development initiative.

The DISSA members pooled their labour efforts in collecting stones and sand for their workshop as opposed to contracting the work out to a construction company. This collective problem solving, through active participation by all members reinforces the value of co-operation. DISSA members have worked hard to acquire the necessary skills and training that were required to prepare their businesses in a well run productive manner. DISSA has had the foresight to train some of its members as instructors enabling them to teach others the appropriate skills in utilising available resources, thus meeting their community's needs for skills development.

LOCAL CONTROL AND MANAGEMENT

In community development process, the collection, analysis, monitoring and evaluation of data, provides information and feedback to progress attained. Equally important is the recognition of ethics in the definition and design of the means by which the community achieves the set goals.

Minimum government involvement (preferably at arm's length) in local community affairs helps avoid the imposition of outside 'agenda' on the community development process. Through local control and management, the community stresses autonomy as a central pillar in achieving local and regional control over economic resources. In this process, the strategy of creating new enterprises that minimise reliance on resources outside the community is important. The ultimate goal of local control and management is the achievement of greater community-based involvement in the local economy.

DISSA's aims and objectives are geared towards mobilisation and utilisation of the community's resources such that the programmes which have been initiated are directed by the group with minimum outside influence. The identification of related problems by the members culminated in an action plan designed and implemented through their efforts, with associated benefits and spill-over for the members of the community respectively. During this process, government involvement has been kept at 'arm's length' and this has enabled the local control and management of the project by DISSA members.

NEW VALUE-BASED PHILOSOPHY

Community development is dynamic and emphasises that the pursuit of individual self-interest is dysfunctional with respect to achieving broader community goals. The sharing of responsibility and occupational flexibility, where everyone is able to contribute through mental and physical efforts encourages a better understanding of the various roles required for the smooth functioning of the community. Furthermore, a generally acceptable philosophy promotes a community sense of belonging and solidarity thereby minimising the problems of divisions and segmentation amongst members.

The philosophy that governed DISSA's activities through the years (self-help based on the traditional community approach) required minimal capital resources and hence utilised the abundant labour resources to their advantage. Given the new capital infusion and formulated programmes it is hard to assess if DISSA will be confronted with a redefinition of their underlying philosophy.

SELF-RELIANCE

A consciousness-raising programme with emphasis on reducing economic interests outside the community ensures a realisation of self-reliance in a community development initiative. Furthermore, the implementation of an import substitution strategy that commences with relatively simple techniques and methods that works towards more sophisticated ones mitigates the outflow of capital from the community. A consideration of trade in surplus as opposed to commodity production and intense capitalisation that deviates from providing basic necessities (i.e., sundry items, food, shelter, clothing, social identity, education and health) facilitates the process of attainment of overall objectives. The trade should also include viable ideas and information that cultivates the community spirit and know-how.

The design of methods with a special focus on local resources, tuned to local demand, has helped DISSA increase production based on appropriate forms of technology, thereby reducing the reliance of the community on outside imports. The blacksmith and carpentry units produce products that are low cost, affordable and directly replace outside goods. Moreover, DISSA maintains a tree nursery (to replant harvested areas and expedite afforestation in others), as a cornerstone in attaining maximum sustainable yield.

CAPACITY BUILDING

Community development succeeds through local development organisations that have the capacity to meet both the short and long-range goals. The development and growth of local skills ensures the creation of a pleasant, sociable and marketable workforce that is capable of meeting the challenges of capital technology. Furthermore, the design of local training programmes and the creation of structures and institutions which are in line with the needs of the community, encourages a more productive utilisation of local resources.

DISSA's strategy in acquiring the necessary applied knowledge and skills, has made possible the development of a local pool of human resources capable of managing and administering local enterprises to the benefit of the whole community. The group is actively involved in training local youth and adults, adding to the community's knowledge base.

EQUITY

The provision of a decent quality of life to all members of the community, in the form of necessary material, social, and cultural needs, is fundamental in a community development process. A system that integrates planned and market mechanisms to produce a mixed economy is a means of equitably distributing community resources. The element of fairness must extend across the entire community social fabric (i.e., women, youth, elderly, the disadvantaged, as well as the physically and mentally challenged).

By sharing resources equally amongst members, the group promotes a sense of fairness that minimises discontent and social friction. Furthermore, surplus funds are re-invested in order to develop an adequate capital stock for sustaining continued production related activities. It is a goal of DISSA to use a portion of future proceeds for use in community programmes specially targeted at those faced with an array of social and economic problems.

LIVING WITHIN ECOLOGICAL LIMITS

Community development recognises that ecological balance must not be overridden by over-capitalisation and exploitation of resources. Natural carrying capacity for the locality should be considered in any long-term planning. Community systems should be planned to minimise adverse effects on living capital and a strong stewardship ethic must be part of any consciousness-raising and education programme. Inter-community co-operation on the management of land, forest, water and other exhaustible resources should address sustainability and regeneration, with the realisation that many environmentally related issues are of a trans-boundary nature.

A development initiative places emphasis on equitable distribution of community resources, with the goal of using resources efficiently and simultaneously reducing the consumption of non-renewable ones. A strategy to move towards renewable "pulsating forms of energy"[25]

---

[25] Pulsating forms of energy refers to sources which are continuous such as the sun and wind.

as a means of synchronising human activity with nature is a necessary part of the development process.

The group's conservation practices, as indicative of the methods applied, gives significance to the value of balancing ecological factors with community needs. Trees from the local nursery have not only been used to replant the productive forest lands but also to enhance soil fertility, reduce soil erosion and promote effective crop and vegetable production. An integrated conservation strategy is well illustrated between the linkage of the local manufacturer of the charcoal stove and the use of waste from the sawmilling operation as fuel. The use of simple methods and tools in the production of crops and forestry have helped minimise the dangers posed by large production techniques (i.e., clear cutting and mechanised farming systems), which are costly in economic and environmental terms.

DIVERSITY

A conscious reduction of uniformity[26], with the goal of achieving diversity in all forms of activity is one of the main goals of community development. Through diversification, the integration of multi-cultural traits broaden a community's perspective in the choice of alternatives and this results in a better way of life for members. The development of a non-cash economy and the informal sector as a means of reducing dependency on the conservatist economic organisation widens the community's economic base. Diversification also means derivation of economic activities that utilise existing local resources with both forward and backward linkages thereby creating more economic opportunities for the community.

The widening of the local community resource base has helped DISSA's programmes create forward linkages (i.e., in the form of marketing and transportation) and backward linkages (i.e., in the form of forestry, crop production and blacksmithing). This economic diversification has shielded DISSA from the vagaries of the commodity market price fluctuations.

---

[26] Uniformity refers to the process whereby monoculture or deliberate reduction of diversity is substituted for processes which involve more spontaneity and creativity.

CO-OPERATION AND COLLABORATION

Community development ensures that inter-community linkages are fostered and co-ordinated in areas of resource management, utilisation and alternative trade. The involvement of all levels of governments to provide support in the form of extension services, enabling legislation and avenues for capital funding are important to achieving the community's set goals. The linking of urban and rural sectors in an inter-dependent relationship (i.e., of equitable sharing of the benefits of successful local development programmes) helps create efficient utilisation of local resources.

Linkages with other institutions (i.e., NGOs, government and other local community groups) has enabled DISSA to overcome the problems associated with low capital stock, limited market access and inadequate technical skill development in the community. In co-operation with these agencies and associations, DISSA has developed strong networks that have fostered appropriate forms of technology, conservation practices, and community relations.

APPROPRIATE INDICATORS

Community development recognises that local programmes should address political, economic, socio-cultural and ecological aspects of the community. The 'yardstick' for measuring development initiatives should include per capita income, as well as socio-political indexes (i.e., environmental impact, waste reduction measures and social harmony). This form of measurement acknowledges that full employment is a necessary part of any development programme, and that all able-bodied adults should contribute to the productive well-being of the community.

While economic development has been an explicit motive of the DISSA project, there has been a realisation that socio-cultural, political, and ecological factors are as important and have to be addressed. The sharing of resources, which puts less pressure on available stocks, facilitates cohesiveness and co-operation that is in line with the Alur cultural traditions.

Conclusion

The motive in analysing the DISSA initiative within the purview of a comprehensive community-based development design is the desire to derive functional and effective methods in project management and development process, which can be used to inform other related projects. It is my conviction that indicators in determining the success of a development process must go well beyond traditional economic cost-benefit analysis to include social, cultural, political, and ecological perspectives.

The approach used in studying this development process revealed that sustained community commitment and involvement cannot be generated or imposed from outside; rather it is evolved from within, with a resultant community will to goal formulation and its attainment. This commitment and involvement is best achieved through a dissemination and information network that provokes the views of the people, thus forming part of the development process.

Through this book it is evident that DISSA's success in achieving their set goals can be attributed to certain key aspects and factors. The group implemented a strategy that accommodated the existing agrarian values and means of production which up to the present moment has been reflected in their produce. DISSA's aims and objectives are compatible with the Uganda government's programme of building an independent self-sustaining and integrated national economy which led to a good working relationship with the government. They established a framework that ensured local community control in their interaction with external agencies. The efforts with which DISSA operated within ecological limits as seen in the methods of conservation, restoration and meeting standards on resource use, indicates their commitment to sustainable practices. DISSA's cohesiveness, through shared responsibility and equity, is instrumental in perpetuating a commitment to their programme. A strong and devoted management team drawn from within the community designed a plan of action that attracted the ADF and other NGO's which facilitated the acquisition of aid in the form of grants and technical assistance.

In spite of DISSA's strengths it should be noted that there are a number of weaknesses, which if are not addressed could lead to problems in the long run. Gender imbalance is evident and the involvement of women is lacking. Information regarding the group's activities and objectives is not reaching the bulk of the community. A protracted community outreach programme in this direction would be appropriate. Lack of effective communication facilities creates slack decision-making process between programme sub-units. Expensive maintenance of machinery and vehicles requires steady economic activity throughout the year to ensure their economic viability. Over-emphasis on economic development aspects poses threats to socio-cultural and political aspects of the community. Finally, DISSA by-laws need a review so that greater community involvement is achieved.

In order to attain a more balanced and sustained community-based development DISSA would need to address the following. First, ways should be found to actively involve more women in the programme. DISSA should act as a role model to change current attitudes towards women's participation and rights. Second, in order to mitigate misinterpretation of the activities by some members in the community, especially the elders, DISSA should pursue a community education programme that would spell out their aims and objectives (channels would include newspapers, radio, newsletters and skits). Third, focus should be placed on reducing maintenance costs of equipment by training their own mechanics and where possible, to produce replacement parts locally. Fourth, there should be more emphasis on community centred development, as opposed to just focusing on the economic aspects. Fifth, values on community ethics, communal accountability and responsibility need to be reinforced.

In summing up, a comparative examination of a community development design with DISSA, a development initiative that suits a description of *community development as institutional initiative* and grounded in the community, has clearly spelled out that a successful community development initiative has its community at the centre of the development process. Genuine community development can only be achieved if control over identification, design and implementation is left in the hands of the very people who stand to benefit from the initiative.

Chapter IV
Community Development Training and Education

This chapter explores in a prescriptive way the connections between community development training and education in the process of implementation and in ensuring the sustainability of a community development initiative. Having examined the DISSA project from a community development perspective, this chapter identifies appropriate training, design and implementation strategies including monitoring and evaluation of the initiative. In addition, when considering that community development aims to institute socio-economic change, it is appropriate to conclude that education, training and organisational initiatives are imperative. Preceding the conclusion of the chapter is a presentation of an effective approach to further investigate and inform the practice of development initiatives.

In Uganda (as in other parts of sub-Sahara Africa), several non-governmental organisations (NGOs), notably church and other local organisations such as business groups, informal groups, informal clans, and community organisations, women and youth groups, farmers' co-operatives, are currently engaged in community development activities (de Coninck, 1992).

There is great diversity among NGOs and local organisations regarding their level of expertise and resources (de Coninck, 1992). For instance, most professional international NGOs operate through a dedicated local staff running selected community development projects. The community development co-ordinators are highly skilful in social animation and follow a participatory planning and management approach with proper physical and financial monitoring mechanisms. Their project work is facilitated by reliable funding and technical backstopping from their overseas headquarters (UNCRD, 1992). A typical NGO – World Vision – practices a holistic development approach where special focus is placed on people's growth of confidence and self-reliance (de Coninck, 1992). As a consequence, they identify with the project activities for which they mobilised their resources and feel responsible for ensuring sustainable project benefits. Using this approach, the NGO provides locally-unavailable resources so as not to undermine self-reliant community development. A community development planning work-book clearly accounts for these resources and contains updated notes on all relevant project aspects (UNCRD, 1992). It thus functions as a practical tool for continuous project monitoring. As part of an overall strategy to build human resource capacity, skilled and motivated community animators are considered as the most valuable resources for local development. Local organisations, in contrast to international NGOs, largely depend on technical backstopping and supplementary resources. Many community projects currently fail due to the lack of information and know-how in mobilising outside assistance.

In sum, community development co-ordinators must be skilled in both community development as well as project management in order to serve as a link between self-help community development activities and public resources (Theobold, 1987). The 'civic entrepreneur' is the leader of exceptional personal vision, able to mobilise resources and apply strategic intuition. With proper training and administrative support, co-ordinators orchestrate the self-help community development activities according to the local planning process.

From the practitioners' perspective, there are four notable steps in community development (UNCRD, 1992). In the first step, an attempt is made to elaborate a realistic picture of the current socio-economic and physical-environmental development of the local situation in the community by developing a local database. The first step concludes with the identification and prioritisation of local needs, problems, and potentials. In the second step, community objectives and targets are set. It is on this basis that the success or failure of project implementation is measured. The third step starts with the identification of project ideas. The prioritisation of project proposals is necessary to determine the rank order for project execution. The last step comprises project execution, monitoring, and evaluation. The creation of such a community development planning process therefore requires an extensive learning process for both local planners and local communities until locally-initiated projects are effectively planned and executed (Fenn, 1989; Ramirez, 1983; UNCRD, 1992). In this regard, community development co-ordinators endeavour to ensure the participation of as many community groups as possible in the planning process. Only when the living conditions of all community groups are gradually improved and a community sense of solidarity is developed, will sustainable local development take place.

Training Approach for Community Development

Training aims to modify or change the behaviour and performance of the training participants and thus contribute to the effectiveness of the organisations for which they work. Training must be systematic and subjected to straightforward planning, innovative implementation, and rigorous evaluation (UNCRD, 1992). The previous analysis of community development planning and management and the recommended planning approach for community development constitute the research diagnosis, as the first stage of the training process. It reveals that the shortage of planning and management capacity largely constrains the introduction of a community development training approach. Training of governmental and non-governmental community development planners thus constitutes a decisive instrument for promoting community development.

Community development co-ordinators and extension workers can be identified as the two target groups[27] of planners and facilitators (Christenson & Jerry, 1989; Blondin, 1971; Clawley, 1989). The community development co-ordinators perform middle management-level tasks, such as giving project planning directives to extension workers, supervising them in the project implementation process, and reporting to senior decision makers. Their training needs thus concentrate on local planning and management skills and techniques, particularly regarding the formulation and appraisal of local project proposals, as well as the monitoring and evaluation of local projects (Sautoy, 1962; UNCRD, 1992). This training can be

---

[27] Target groups for training in local planning and management include: project co-ordinators and their supervisors, government extension workers, community representatives and leaders (youth, women's groups, business leaders, students, retired but active civil servants, and pastors((UNCRD, 1992: p.21).

undertaken in a classroom base, supplemented by short visits to project sites.

The extension workers execute local projects in close interaction with communities. Community representatives and leaders are included in this target group because they are instrumental in mobilising communal resources and organising community activities (Beal et al, 1966; Knowles, 1980). The training emphasis is therefore on skills and techniques in both local planning and management as well as community development. The training is conducted at district and county level, with a strong emphasis on field-management tasks, and where selected local communities are assisted in a specific planning and management task, such as the preparation of a community profile or the prioritisation of local problems and needs.

At a third stage of the training process, objectives and targets have to be set. In DISSA the overall long-term training objective required an upgrade of the local planning and management capacity with a strategy of improving the community's living conditions. More specific long-term objectives would include an increase in the ratio of locally-initiated micro-projects; to improve the sustainability of local projects already initiated; to consider adequate maintenance and depreciation costs in the preparation of project budgets; and to enhance the collaboration between NGOs, local community organisations, and the government in community development.

Immediate training objectives specify the particular skills and techniques to be transferred to the community development planners; for instance, to formulate a consistent local project proposal; to undertake a simple financial or feasibility analysis of a local project proposal; to apply the various scheduling methods for the project activities and other related activities (UNCRD, 1992). The evaluation of the training programme would reveal whether the local planners have acquired these skills and techniques. The achievement of the immediate training objectives, however, does not necessarily lead to the fulfilment of long-term objectives, because the institutional and socio-cultural settings determine whether the local planners will be capable and motivated to apply the newly acquired skills and techniques to their actual work assignments (UNCRD, 1992).

The design of the training programme constitutes a fourth stage of the training process (UNCRD, 1992). Design of the training programme for the community development co-ordinators is based on four premises[28]. Very important areas include the elaboration of a concept for a course, the development of reading materials and exercises, the selection and assignment of resource persons to both conduct the course and prepare training materials, nominate participants, and identify training tools and facilities (Tough, 1975; Knowles, 1980; Nadler, 1982).

The fifth stage of the training process is conducting the training courses. Methods used to conduct the training vary depending on the academic and experience level of the participants and the form the initiative takes (i.e., as a process, method, institutional initiative or movement). Consequently, the other perspectives of training are dictated by the nature of development, for instance, conservative or radical, classical or romantic (Jarvis, 1985); a collection of courses or integrated (Jarvis, 1985); pedagogical or androgogical (Knowles, 1980); a reproduction of knowledge or a transformation of it (Griffin, 1983); domesticating or liberating (Freire, 1970); operational or intrinsic (Brookfield, 1986). Although this diversity of approaches poses a problem for the training programme planner, the most important factor for community development initiatives is the context in which a curriculum is developed (Giroux, 1983).

The evaluation of the training courses, as the sixth and final stage of the training process, is undertaken by the participants to indicate if the programme was worthwhile. From a social action and co-operative extension perspective, the total programme evaluation is only one of the many steps in the entire process of the development of the training programme. The evaluation process operates a formative evaluation check on each stage of the training programme and is later applied in the summative evaluation at the end of programme (Beal et al, 1966). This process has implications for future programming (e.g., it indicates whether the training content was of direct relevance to work

---

[28] The premises are: 1) the elaboration of relevant and comprehensible training materials, based on field research within the project location, allowing the participants to relate the course contents directly to their work assignments; 2) the focus on group exercises and preliminary sessions, with minimum time for lectures, stimulates the interaction between local and government officers, as well as project co-ordinators; 3) the various group exercises on selected planning steps, such as the prioritisation of problems, the setting of objectives, and the formulation of a whole project proposal, involve the participants in the process of integrating action and reflection; and 4) the involvement of senior government officials in selected course sessions is likely to strengthen the motivation of the participants (UNCRD, 1992: p.18).

settings; if the duration of the course needs to be prolonged; whether undertaking the training demands much closer assistance by senior training instructors; or if there is a need for a follow-up training course after programme completion).

Importance of the Training Design

The aim of training designs on community development and management is to systematically explain the main steps of local planning processes and to describe simple and straightforward planning techniques related to the development initiative (UNCRD, 1992). Training designs attempt to reduce the complexity of the general planning process to the minimum. They focus on the planning and implementation process for local projects within the socio-economic and cultural setting of the project. Their only aim is to cover planning skills and techniques of practical value for the local planners, illustrated with case examples of local projects within such a project site. They must be based on an intimate understanding of local or rural people to undertake community development in the project environment (Uma, 1975).

Although community development planning and implementation are not necessarily sequential, the rational approach to training based on the following four considerations provide guidance for a planner; a) exclusive focus is given to local projects – omitting the formulation and implementation of local programmes and a development plan – which are considered key instruments to bring about improvements in local or rural living conditions in the light of the current planning and management capacity. Emphasis is thereby given to an inter-sectoral approach to project planning and management. b) similarly, there is no urgent need for the formulation of local development strategies as long as community development initiatives are consistent with local, provincial, and national development objectives and responsive to local needs and priorities. c) community development initiatives financing emphasises the preparation of a sound project budget by cashflow and profit-loss analyses as a crucial component of a development initiative proposal and d) the choice of a community development initiative cannot be adequately covered by a module because an institutional framework for the selection and negotiation process for local projects are impacted on by the socio-political and economic conditions that prevail at the time (UNCRD, 1992).

Community development planning and implementation process in practice is not linear as suggested by many planning models. As was observed in DISSA the concurrent and sometimes interchangeable operation of the carpentry and joinery with blacksmith units is a good illustration. They can take place at the same time, in a different order, or they can be completely bypassed, as is particularly the case with project evaluation. Nevertheless, the integrated project cycle[29] is a suitable concept for both training and the actual process of project planning and implementation (UNCRD, 1992). It can lead to a more systematic decision-making process in project planning and management compared to the ad hoc decision-making process.

Planning and Management of Community Development

In community development there is a need to integrate theory and practice in the planning process. Community development planning should link overall objectives with the action and process (Dykeman, 1988). It is thus important to have a well managed training programme.

In regard to planning, an analysis of the local situation occurs through a systematic process of examining and understanding the socio-economic, cultural, political, administrative and physical-environmental conditions in a selected local planning area as well as the outside factors which affect the locality in question (So, 1984). This is relevant where outside factors with a decisive impact on local living conditions may override any local control (i.e., increases in prices of essential commodities, such as gasoline, rice, salt, and detergents). Furthermore, unanticipated declines in prices for cash crops such as cassava, coffee, cotton, maize and simsim greatly affect local cash income opportunities. This analysis tries to gain useful insights into the people's current living conditions and how

---

[29] The concept of integrated project cycle emphasises the interdependent and cyclical nature of projects as will as their linear progression, where each planning set is distinct and proceeds in an orderly time sequence. It perceives project development as the systematic development of a project idea for the eventual objective of arriving at an investment decision.

they can be improved or changed to achieve local objectives and targets.

It is the first stage of the community development process which enables the community development co-ordinator to begin defining problems affecting the local planning area, and to determine the resources required to effect the desired changes. It also provides the basis for projecting into the future using methods of forecasting and analysis. In addition, it provides the initial opportunity for involving local people in the planning process (Beal et al, 1966; Seasons, 1979; Fenn, 1989).

The data collected at this stage is used in a number of ways throughout the local planning process. The data is used to identify local needs and problems as well as to justify proposals for local projects. Furthermore, the data should be used as a 'base-line' for the monitoring and evaluation of the projects concerned.

The analysis of the local situation must be systematic in order to get a clear understanding of the nature of the communities concerned because each community is unique and the local planner must thus be open to the particular characteristics, perspectives and problems of each. Most importantly, the analysis of the local situation must be an open and participatory process because communities are often far from homogenous. Representatives from all community groups should thus participate in the interpretation of the data collected (Robert, 1974; Steiner, 1979; Lang, 1988; Seasons, 1988; Filion, 1988).

Techniques chosen for data gathering must be suitable to the planning effort. The kind of data collection is often determined by budgeting constraints as well as by the role local people play in the data collection process. The local planner must always be concerned with the cost-effectiveness of the data collection process (Bowles, 1981; So, 1984). There is often a tendency to collect too much unnecessary data in the process.

When resources are disbursed for the conduct of a survey, the survey should be designed and utilised during and after a first round of talks between the community co-ordinator, community leaders and the ordinary people (UNCRD, 1992). A survey could then provide not only information about the incidence and causes of particular problems and needs but it could also explore people's skills, resources and reactions to possible alternatives for dealing with them.

As alternatives begin to be defined, it may also be possible to explore the feasibility of proposed projects. According to the United Nations Centre for Rural Development (1992), information that is required includes a) information on the resources needed to make projects workable; b) an inventory of available community resources and expertise, such as labour, materials, land, donation of food, housing; c) estimate of community ability to procure these resources if they are not available locally; d) anticipated problems in actually carrying out projects; e) the anticipated role of local meetings and officials in implementing whatever approaches chosen; and f) what kind of projects have been tried in the community in the past and what happened to them.

From the foregoing argument, it is important that analysis of the local situation must point out all significant features under community existing circumstances from which project characteristics are developed. It is only after this consideration that the situational analysis can serve as a proper precondition for a higher rate of successful local projects (Steiner, 1979; Lang, 1988; Filion, 1988). Good understanding is required on the part of the local planner for designing a workable situational analysis and for interpretation of the data gathered.

Once local needs and potentials have been identified, the community concerned has to set local objectives and targets (UNCRD, 1992). Relating to the DISSA experience this includes spelling out local objectives and development aims within a given time-frame. In other words, it describes how the community would like to see the existing undesirable conditions improved. A local target specifies the type of output necessary for achieving the local objective concerned. It spells out the operations within a given time-frame needed to bring about the desired improvements (UNCRD, 1992).

The setting of local objectives and targets by community members is often a difficult political process which requires mediation skills from the local community development co-ordinator (Christenson & Jerry 1989). The community development evaluation should be as open as possible in order to facilitate the participation of all groups and segments of the community. Nevertheless, the local planner should be aware of the power struggle among community members because powerful people are likely to influence others (Warner, 1989; Cervero & Wilson, 1994). Disadvantaged groups like the very poor or minorities may have little energy and confidence to express their views. It is important to ensure that setting local objectives and targets is a fair process requiring a mechanism that reflects an equitable distribution of resources and one that maintains the commitment of various groups to collective activities (UNCRD, 1992). Equally important are cases where problems mentioned by community members may all relate to some underlying, basic issue that is critical to the community. For instance, problems of malnutrition, poor health and children who work rather than go to school may all be traced back to insufficient income and employment opportunities. Therefore, in the local community development planning process it is essential to focus on significant problems that impinge on the overall objective.

Implementation Process for Community Development

The purpose of the community development planning process is to design local initiatives which can be carried out effectively. Planning is necessary to guide the implementation process. Owing to uncertainties of the project environment, planning must be flexible in order to adapt to unanticipated situations that occur during the implementation process.

The community development co-ordinator has two primary roles in the process of implementing the community development initiative: firstly, he/she takes part in the development initiative design process by spelling out the steps required for execution, such as determining exactly what needs to be done, in what order, by whom and using what materials and methods (Christenson & Jerry, 1989; Warner, 1989). Secondly, he/she may manage or monitor the actual development initiative execution as project co-ordinator. Furthermore, the community development co-ordinator may be involved in evaluating the development initiative upon completion.

Development initiative design, monitoring and evaluation are closely related components of the implementation process (UNCRD, 1992). The design includes a schedule which clearly illustrates the timing and duration of all activities planned for the overall implementation process. The monitoring process utilises the development initiative schedule during the actual implementation process to check whether the project activities are on schedule. When problems arise, they can immediately be identified and rectified. Once the development initiative is implemented, evaluation is concerned with determining whether or not the project has actually been a success and why (Christenson & Jerry, 1989).

Analogous to the development initiative planning process, it is essential that members of the target group(s) actively participate in the whole implementation process (Cernea, 1981). In addition, formal and informal local organisations are necessary to assume responsibilities as well as serving as a communication bridge between the people and the community development co-ordinator (Hodge & Qadeer, 1983). Local organisations have to be created for a participatory project planning and implementation process to start. This takes a long time and requires the local planner to work directly with the people on a day-to-day basis (Warner, 1981; UNCRD, 1992).

While rational planning seems appealing to the design of training and implementation processes, the approach has potential weaknesses that planners need to consider (Adams, 1991). As an approach that is 'expert driven' there is a danger of thwarting opinions or views from practitioners who are themselves not experts. Community development initiatives are participatory and works on the notion of 'by-us for-us' rather than 'by-them for-us'.

The rational approach places great emphasis on success and has more regard for intended rather than unintended outcomes in its entire process (Adams, 1991). The weakness posed in this case is that community development is a process which encompasses broad socio-political and economic strata of society. The approach predetermines its definition of success and strives to measure the outcome against it. In the practical world, community is dynamic and changes, for instance, in political priority and community aspirations are resisted in the rational domain due to its lack of flexibility.

Adams further argues that the approach applies a "top-down, centralised and hierarchical" system in its implementation. Community development settings are dynamic, most of the initiatives are grass-roots based, are based on a bottom-up process, and participants-instructors have a learner-learner relationship. It is therefore useful, as Adams suggests, for community development planners and co-ordinators to expand their planning approaches to include consensual and political approaches[30].

Monitoring Community Development Initiatives

Community development monitoring, as the collection, analysis and presentation of data, enables the co-ordinator to assess the progress of the initiative and to take timely decisions to ensure that it is maintained according to schedule (UNCRD, 1992). As an integral part of day-to-day management it is the primary responsibility of the co-ordinator to know and to adapt to what is actually happening in the field (Wade, 1989; Cawley, 1989). Monitoring community development emphasises periodic review of the implementation schedule in order to measure inputs, activities and outputs undertaken during the implementation process. The implementation schedule has to be checked against implementation progress. Development initiative monitoring should be considered a learning process because most critical lessons are learned during the implementation process and the implementation schedule must be adjusted to take them into account (Littrell & Hobbs, 1989; UNCRD, 1992).

Methods for monitoring community development initiatives combine the information system with administrative mechanisms (UNCRD, 1992). In other words, if the information system indicates delays or bottlenecks of scheduled activities, immediate actions must be started in order to overcome bottlenecks or minimise delays. The implementation schedule is accordingly modified to allow for continuous monitoring. The development initiative information system must consist of data that is easily collectable at periodic intervals during the implementation process. It also consists of base-line data collected during the situational analysis that is needed to assess changes of certain community conditions over a specific period of time. More importantly, every part of the information system should

---

[30] Adams argues that planning is in a crisis if it does not address the questions of definition, intellectual or scientific foundation, success and ideology. To him the solution is found in an intersection of the political, consensual and technicist, within the larger framework of Interactive and Rational Educational Planning. (Adams, 1991: p.13).

be timely, reliable, relevant and action-oriented (Robert, 1974; UNCRD, 1992).

The data needs for community development monitoring are determined by the initiative targets which specify the intended outcomes. Information on the provision of inputs can be accessed from extension workers, health workers, instructors and construction supervisors. The more simple and straightforward the information systems, the more reliable they are. They can also be supplemented with field visits by the community development co-ordinator (UNCRD, 1992). The information and results of the reporting systems should be communicated to the target group(s) so that their conclusions and priorities can be reflected in the continuing project implementation process. The dissemination of project information between project staff and beneficiaries must be an ongoing process (Beal et al, 1966).

The administrative mechanisms for project monitoring are regular community development meetings and action reports. A project meeting should be held every week or month depending on the project schedule (Warner, 1989). It should be held in the local community concerned in order to facilitate the participation of the local community members in the project implementation process (Robert, 1974). All people involved in project execution should report their activities and problems encountered during the previous week or month and lay out their activities planned for the coming week or month. During the monitoring process, community members can be encouraged to suggest ideas and solutions to the implementation problems faced (UNCRD, 1992). Depending on the degree of deviation between the work schedule and implementation progress, necessary changes and modifications should be mutually discussed, decided and acted upon.

Evaluation of Community Development Initiatives

Evaluation is an ongoing process that commences from the project inception to the stage when all benefits are expected to have been realised. It assesses the overall impact of the development initiative – including intentional and unintentional outcomes– on the beneficiaries in particular, as well as on the entire community (UNCRD, 1992). Community development evaluation is a process for systematically and objectively determining relevance, efficiency, effectiveness and impact. This is measured against the development initiative's original objectives, thereby discovering whether all were met and if not, where and why they could not be met (Christenson & Jerry, 1989). It draws conclusions and implications that are useful in the post-development initiative activities including the planning and execution of new and similar initiatives. According to the United Nations Centre for Rural Development (1992), the purpose of evaluation is to facilitate; a) an identification of those constraints and bottlenecks which could not be anticipated during the planning process; b) the delineation of project benefits and costs; c) an examination of organisational mechanisms and procedures in the planning and implementation process; d) a determination of the reasons for which the project schedule had to be altered; e) an assessment of the degree to which the target groups have actually benefited from the project; and f) a documentation of experiences and results from which recommendation can be formulated for similar projects.

The timing of the evaluation is important because the sustainability of an initiative can only be determined when the long-term project impact is realised. The timing varies a lot from initiative to initiative and a successfully executed development initiative can be considered a failure due to unexpected changes (UNCRD, 1992). For instance, new agricultural technologies may change in the long run the division of labour at the family or household level, with negative or positive repercussions on community life. Such changes are captured by the evaluation process.

The responsibility to carry out community development evaluation can either be assigned to the community co-ordinator and his/her staff or outside evaluators from an independent organisation, such as a research institute or a consulting firm or evaluators from the funding agency, or to a joint team comprising the project manager and outside evaluators (UNCRD, 1992). In this process, Deshler (1984) cautions that it is no longer acceptable for practitioners or evaluators to apply to everything the one approach with which they are familiar. In addition to this caution, it is imperative for the people involved to decide how and to what extent the target group(s) and the whole local community can participate in the evaluation process (Robert, 1974). Although more objectivity and experiences are expected from outside evaluators, a potential weakness they possess is the lack of any direct experience and communication links with the target group(s) (Knowles, 1980; UNCRD, 1992). This situation renders a joint evaluation team of the community, the development co-ordinator, his/her staff and one or two experienced outside evaluators an ideal provided that they collaborate according to mutually agreed terms of reference. As part of community development practice of sharing experience, a sensitive outside evaluator can enrich the discussions by bringing in experiences, perspectives and dimensions which may have been overlooked by the project staff and the local community. By asking constructive questions in a sensitive way, the outside evaluator may help the project staff and the local community to realise and address unpleasant facts and sensitive problems which may otherwise undermine the sustainability of the development initiative (UNCRD, 1992).

A self-evaluation by community development workers is another feasible approach that was undertaken for the DISSA project. In a first step, the method of participatory evaluation needs to be discussed with the group. In the second step, the staff will be provided with background reading materials and guidelines for preparing a case study of their component. In a third step, the case studies will be edited and distributed to the participants of the evaluation workshop. In a fourth step, the evaluation workshop will be conducted comprising the discussion of the project case studies and field visits to the project area(s). Lastly, conclusions and recommendations have to be elaborated and formulated for a joint evaluation report (UNCRD, 1992).

Evaluation process should take place in the local planning area in order to allow for the participation of community members. The purpose of the evaluation must be clearly explained and accepted by the local community. It is only in an atmosphere of collaboration and confidence, that reliable information is gathered. Therefore, it is essential for outside evaluators to get a first-hand impression of what has actually happened in comparison to what the project proclaims to have achieved (UNCRD, 1992).

From the above argument the evaluation process should be conducted by and for the people most involved in the development initiative. This is because the evaluation process itself is as important as the conclusions drawn. It is the participation aspect that induces a better understanding of development initiative activities and a more constructive approach to post-development action, should it be required (UNCRD, 1992). The evaluation methods should therefore not exceed the skills and understanding of the community development workers and the community members. If they were able to undertake a community profile, they can use a base-line data for community development evaluation. The findings of the evaluation process should be presented in an understandable format and language during a community meeting in order to incorporate recommendations from community members in the evaluation report.

In conclusion, a suitable approach to community development assessment is participatory evaluation. As a long-term ongoing process it is based on dialogue between community members, the development workers and outside evaluators. It is this continuous dialogue that strengthens local relationships and networks and ultimately creates a climate of confidence in which feedback and constructive criticism can be accepted. The continuous dialogue enables the community members, the development workers and the outside evaluators to reflect on their experiences with the development undertaken in order to improve it or to incorporate the experiences from a completed development into future planning and implementation. In other words, participatory evaluation is a continuous learning process of action and reflection.

Community Development and Further Investigation

Within a given community development setting, it is of interest to seek understanding of the situation, how it was addressed, and what lessons, if any, can be learned for future ventures. A research approach that can appropriately lead to this explanation is participatory research (PR). Participatory research is most commonly described as an integrated activity that combines social investigation, educational work and action. The combination of the basic characteristics of the research approach and interrelationships presented by Hall (1984) could be summarised thus: research should involve people in the entire process; research should result in some direct and positive benefits for those communities and people involved; research is a process of knowledge creation which may or may not involve professionally-trained researchers; knowledge is deepened, enriched, and made more socially usable when it is produced collectively;

research involves a combination of methods designed to facilitate social, co-operative, or collective production of knowledge; and research, learning, and knowledge production are often aspects of the same intellectual processes in the context of action.

By its nature, participatory research offers a strategy for local training and education, research and organisation and planning that is consistent with the assumptions of people-centred development (Brown, 1985). To this effect interventions that grow out of participatory research are locally developed and managed. Local community members define problems, analyse alternative solutions, choose action strategies and implement the chosen strategies. The members are trained to organise themselves to take appropriate action. It encourages inquiry that focuses on local problems and pragmatic concerns, it provides education that encourages active involvement and informal collective action and it builds organisations that enable cohesive local action and links groups to the larger political and economic context (Hall, 1984; Brown, 1985). Participatory research, as Brown cautions, is a micro-strategy most relevant to mobilisation and development at the local level, but the larger context of political, economic, and cultural patterns can facilitate or impede this type of research.

Participatory research is appropriate in community development especially for programmes with similar characteristics to DISSA. This is due to its emphasis on involvement of the poor and the 'exploited' in the research process itself; a shift in the location of the research from developed countries to the Third World and its greater preference for local researchers to expatriates. By implication, participatory research develops organisations – not just knowledge and educated individuals but also their ability to act more effectively at the local level.

Chapter V
Conclusion

This book has presented a literature review on the body of work that espouses the notion of community development. The author concurs with the view that community development remains a useful mechanism for the alleviation of socio-economic problems facing most Third World communities.

The book has confirmed that community development expresses itself in several forms (i.e., as a method, a process, an institutional initiative and a social movement). The author agrees that despite this diversity in forms, community development initiatives share common elements that enable each and every form to fit under the umbrella term community development. The elements include local community participation in decision-making and planning; a focus on local initiative and leadership development through skills training and education; the endeavour for self-help and self-reliance; a belief in co-operation and collaboration within and outside of the community; optimum utilisation of local resources; the raising of community consciousness and empowerment, and local control over community resources.

The author has noted that while community development principles and expressions are easily understood, several factors impede the effective implementation of development initiatives. The obstacles in the community include: resentment to planning due to negative experiences with public officials, deficient knowledge about community potential and opportunities, and the lack of training in community development theories, techniques and practices. As part of its conclusion, the book emphasises the need to train and educate community members on community development techniques and practices as well as other factors that ensure community competitiveness amidst scarce resources from the public purse.

Chapter III of the book has undertaken a careful examination of community development with DISSA, a Third World development initiative which suits a description of *community development as institutional initiative*. DISSA is an adult-youth initiative that is grounded in the community. As is clearly manifested in DISSA, successful community development initiatives require its community to be at the centre stage of the entire development process. In addition, sustainable community development is best achieved when control over identification, design, and implementation is left in the hands of the very people who stand to benefit from the initiative.

Mention was made by the author regarding limitations of in-depth book on DISSA. The information presented was generated from the responses in the survey questionnaire that was mailed from Vancouver, Canada to DISSA executive committee members in Nebbi, Uganda, together with the project appraisal documents and photograph collections. The author agreed that although he was born and raised in the vicinity of DISSA's geographic location, a field trip, with an observer-as-participant approach and interviews (as additional forms of data collection) could have augmented the book.

In Chapter IV, the book noted the necessity of pursuing training and education for the achievement of sustainable community development. The author also shared the view that community development is an evolving and ongoing process. It requires that skills are continually transformed in order to face the challenges of development. In this regard, the book examined the ways in which learning theories are applied in sharing skills and knowledge in the context of community development. The author's motive in analysing learning theories as to their suitability in communicating the skills amongst community development groups was the desire to establish how the process of adult learning could be strengthened.

The author further argued that training and education aim to modify or change the behaviour and performance of participants, and thus contribute to the effectiveness of the organisations to which they are connected. Such training must be systematic and subjected to straightforward planning, innovative implementation and rigorous evaluation. In sum, community development co-ordinators must be skilled in both community development as well as project management techniques in order to effectively serve as a link between self-help community development activities and the external world.

While rational approaches to planning and implementation processes are espoused by the author, practitioners are cautioned of the potential weaknesses posed. They include the approach's over-emphasis on predetermined measurement of success; a top-down, expert led approach; and the lack of addressing both intended and unintended outcomes to planning. Planning literature does, however, suggest the application of an approach that regards both the interactive and rational domains thereby intersecting the three zones of consensual, technicist and political.

For further investigation in the field of community development, the author regards participatory research as one of the most suitable. This is due to its emphasis on the involvement of beneficiaries in the research process. Finally, the author notes that participatory research develops organisations – not just knowledgeable and educated individuals – but also their ability to act more effectively at the local community level.

Appendix A

Survey Questionnaire: Community Economic Development Study on DISSA Youth Development Initiative

A: Historical Information

1. What were the traditional ways prior to foreign contact? (i.e. economic, social, political, ritual, cultural practices.)

2. What were the prominent features of the local economy just prior to the community development strategy?

3. What were the roots to your community problems?

4. What prompted the community to explore alternative development strategies?

5. What were identified as the potential economic opportunities in your region?

6. What is the underlying philosophy by which you have approached the community development process?

B: Project Implementation

1. Why was this particular development process chosen?

2. What were the aims and objectives of your development strategy?

3. Has this development strategy had spin-off effects in neighbouring communities? If so, in what manner?

4. What are your ties with other organisations (i.e. non-governmental organisations, governments, interest groups, etc.)?

5. What legal arrangements and agreements were required to get the project off the ground?

6. What initial government support did you receive in the development of the project?

7. What have been the major obstacles in implementing your development strategy?

8. State any services which the project brought to the community? (i.e. medical clinic, schools, training facilities, etc.)

9. Are you using a holistic approach (i.e. considering the long term consequences of your development plans)? Please elaborate.

10. Explain where applicable how the project has either influenced or been influenced by the following factors:

> Agriculture
> Education
> Transportation
> Health
> Communications
> Housing
> Land use

11. Has the programme you have undertaken led to regional support and co-operation with neighbouring communities? If so, please explain in what ways.

C: Economic Information

1. What were the mechanisms by which you carried out your objectives (i.e. co-operatives, community development corporations, etc.)?

2. How self-sustaining is your development plan (i.e. does it require outside technical assistance and financial support)?

3. How has capital been secured for your development strategy?

4. If grants or loans were obtained, how long did it take to process them and what qualifications were required?

5. Are project inputs local or imported? Explain and indicate in either case, the types of goods and services provided?

6. If imported inputs are currently being used to what extent are you planning to develop substitutes in the future?

7. What are your expenses? Please indicate the amounts for a specified time period (i.e. semi-annually or annually).

8. What types of training have your people had to undertake in order to acquire the necessary skills and technical knowledge to carry out the various projects your development plan has envisioned?

9. What types of products are you currently producing and what would you like to produce in future?

10. Indicate current prices and main markets of products produced in the community.

11. Are price levels for these products reasonably stable or do they fluctuate depending on the season, etc.? Explain.

12. How do your products reach the market?

13. What methods are used to develop natural resources? Please give detailed explanation of the production process.

14. Are your initiatives yielding community equity and capital accumulation? If so, how is this surplus being utilised?

15. How equitably has income from the community development projects been distributed?

D: Ecological Information

1. What steps have been taken to ensure resource renewal is well managed and that the development plans include overall sustainable yield criteria?

2. How has conservation, sustainability, and good resource management practices influenced your decisions?

3. Has there been a conscious effort to implement techniques which minimise disturbance to the natural environment? If so, what are they and how have they been applied?

4. Have conservation standards been set (either by government or by the project itself)? And if so could you provide details as to what they are?

E: Social And Cultural Information

1. What is the relationship between traditional methods and 'modern' techniques?

2. Has development proceeded in a way that has respected local culture, customs, beliefs, ethics, etc.? What steps have been taken to facilitate these needs?

3. How has development of the programme affected community solidarity and morale?

4. What impact has the project had in deterring migration of capital and people from your community to urban centres? Explain how.

F: Geographical Information

1. (a) Land base of community including (prior to the development initiatives): common property, private property and state owned (please state each type in hectares).
   (b) After implementation of development initiatives:

2. (a) Extractive resource base in hectares (prior to development initiatives): (please identify use, i.e. forests, waterways, agricultural land, etc.).
   (b) After implementation of development initiatives:

4. (a) How were these resources utilised prior to development initiatives?
   (b) After development initiatives:

5. Have detailed inventory data collection of the territory's assets and resources been conducted and if so how was this achieved? (i.e. mapping, surveys, appraisals, etc.)

G: Political Information

1. Describe the development administrative structure. An organisational flow chart may be an effective way of showing this.

2. What role has consciousness-raising played in the success of your community's development process?

3. How was the decision making process conducted?

4. What difficulties have been encountered in the decision-making process?

5. Have there been any problems over user rights and/or ones of jurisdictional nature? If so, what are they?

6. How have senior government responded to any local control initiatives you may have pursued?

7. How have the people in the community participated in your development process? (Indication by gender and age would be helpful.)

8. Has there been a commitment from the start to make this a participatory process? If so, has this been facilitated and how successful has it been?

9. Has there been efforts made to ensure women are included at each phase of development? If so, what are they?

H: Demographic Information

1. Name of community.

2. Names of clan groups.

3. Name of tribal groups.

4. (a) Community population (prior to development initiative):
   (b) Community population (current).

5. Female population: ages 0-12, 13-17, 18-29, 30-49, and 50+ (Note, if these groupings are inconvenient please feel free to alter or omit groupings).

6. Male population: ages 0-12, 13-17, 18-29, 30-49, and 50+ (Note, if these groupings are inconvenient please feel free to alter or omit groupings).

7. Educational level in terms of literacy, skill development (traditional and contemporary), etc. (please specify by gender and age).
   (a) Before development initiative:
   (b) After development initiative.

8. (a) Livelihoods prior to community development initiatives females over the age of 16: (i.e. teachers, clerical, administrative, work in home, agricultural labour, manufacturing, handicrafts, etc.).
   (b) After developmental initiatives:

9. Disparity of real family income between status groups (expressed in terms of weekly consumption of basic goods [i.e. food, clothing, etc.]).
   (a) Prior to development initiatives:
   (b) After development initiatives:

10. (a) Incidence rate of social delinquencies (i.e. substance abuse, suicide, prostitution, family violence, teen pregnancies, theft, etc.) prior to development initiatives.
    (b) After development initiatives.

11. Dependence on government transfers (i.e. unemployment, social assistance, etc.)
    (a) Prior to development initiatives:
    (b) After development initiatives.

I: Project Evaluation Information

1. Has the project helped to alleviate the side effects of the structural adjustment programme set by the IMF? (i.e. currency devaluation, reduction of public expenditure on health and education, privatisation of state owned enterprises, etc.)

2. Does the project have a need for technology transfer from developed countries?

3. From your understanding of development how would you consider this project to be different from other development projects you are familiar with.

4. What have been the key factors in your development process?

5. What do you see as strengths and weaknesses of the particular development strategy you have initiated?

6. What lessons have you learned that might be useful for other communities planning development along these lines?

7. If you could do it over again what would you do differently?

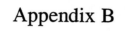

Appendix B

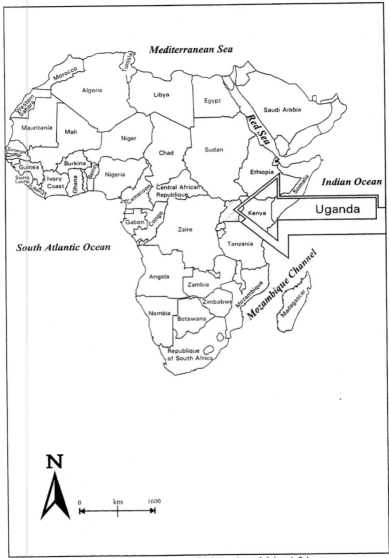

Fig.1: The location of Uganda within Africa

Fig.2: Map of Uganda showing administrative boundaries

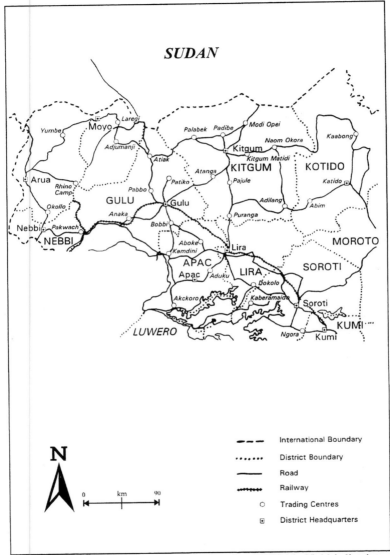

Fig.3: Map of Northern Uganda showing DISSA's Nebbi district

Fig. 4: DISSA Management Flow Chart

DISSA Integrated Rural Development Programme

COMPONENT: SAWMILLING; TRANSPORT; TRADE;
CARPENTRY/BLACKSMITH WORKSHOP

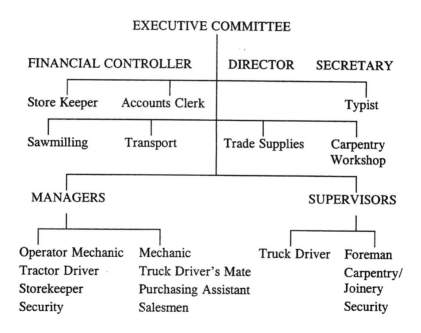

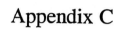

Appendix C

TABLE I

The Distribution of Tribes Among the Four Major Ethnic Groups

Tribes	Number	Percentage of Total African Population
Bantu		
Baganda	1,044,878	16.3
Banyankole	519,283	8.1
Basoga	501,921	7.8
Bakiga	459,619	7.1
Banyaruanda	378,656	5.9
Bagisu	329,257	5.1
Batoro	208,300	3.3
Banyoro	188,374	2.9
Barundi	138,749	2.2
Bagwere	111,681	1.7
Bakonjo	106,890	1.7
Banyole	92,642	1.4
Basamia	47,759	0.7
Bagwe	36,130	0.6
Baamba	34,506	0.5
Bakenyi	23,707	0.4
Batwa	2,592	0.0
TOTAL	4,224,944	65.7
Nilotic		
Lango	363,807	5.6
Acholi	284,929	4.4
Alur	123,378	1.9
Badama	101,451	1.6
Jonam	27,422	0.4
TOTAL	938,635	13.9
Sudanic		
Lugbara	236,270	3.7
Madi	80,355	1.2
Lendu	4,744	1.1
TOTAL	321,369	6.0
Nilo-Hamitic		
Iteso	524,716	8.1
Karamojong	131,713	2.0
Kuman	61,459	1.0
Kakwa	37,628	0.6
Sebei	36,800	0.6
Pokot (suk)	21,850	0.3
Labwor	10,042	0.1
Tepeth	4,363	0.0
TOTAL	828,711	12.7

References

Adams, D., 'Planning Models and Paradigms', ed. R.V. Carlson & G. Awkerman, *Educational Planning: Concepts, Strategies and Practices*, New York, Longman, 1991

Allan, T., Carmichael, B., Karimjee, K., *Evaluation Report of The Ketane Integrated Rural Development Project* (Mohale's Hoek District, Lesotho), Unitarian Service Committee of Canada, 1993

Ameyaw, S., 'Sustainable Development and the Community: Lessons from the Kasha Project' in *Environmentalist*, Botswana, 1992, vol.XII, no.4

Beal, G.M., Blount, R.C, Powers, R.C. & Johnson, W.J., *Social Action and Interaction in Program Planning*, Ames, Iowa State University Press, 1966

Ben-David Val, A., *Local Economic Development Planning: From Goals to Projects*, Chicago, American Planning Association, 1980

Bergman, E., 'Local Economic Development in Era of Capital Mobility' in *Community Planning*, 1981, vol.VII, no.2

Bergman, E. and Goldstein, H., 'Dynamics and Structural Change in Metropolitan Economies' in *Journal of the American Planning Association*, summer 1983

Bibi, T., UNCRD, 'Building Local Institutional Capability and Strengthening Local Autonomy for Local Self-Reliance' in *Sustaining Self-Reliant Local-Level Development in Eastern and Southern Africa*, Harare, Zimbabwe, 1990

Blakely, E. and Bradshaw, T., 'New Roles for Community Developers in Rural Growth Communities' in *Journal of the Community Development Society*, 1982, vol.XIII, no.2

Boone, E., *Developing Programs in Adult Education*, Englewood Cliffs, NJ, Prentice Hall, 1985

102

Bowles, R.T., *Social Impact of Assessment in Small Communities*, Toronto, Butterworths, 1981

Boyle, P., *Planning Better Programs*, New York, McGraw Hill, 1981

Brookfield, S.D., *Understanding and Facilitating Adult Learning*, San Francisco, Jossey-Bass, 1986

Brown, D., 'People-Centred Development and Participatory Research' in *Harvard Educational Review*, February 1985, vol.LV, no.1

Bryant, C.R. and Preston, R.E., *A Framework for Local Initiatives in Economic Development, Economic Development*, Waterloo, Ontario, Economic Development Program, Faculty of Environmental Studies, University of Waterloo, 1987, bulletin no.1

Bryant, C.R. and Preston, R.E., *Strategic Economic Planning and Local Development*, Waterloo, Ontario, Economic Development Program, Faculty of Environmental Studies, University of Waterloo, 1987

Burcell, R. and Listokin, D., *The Fiscal Impact Handbook: Estimating Local Costs and Revenues of Land Development*, Piscataway, NJ, The Centre for Urban Policy Research, 1983

Candy, P., *Mirrors of the Mind: Personal Construct Theory in the Training of Adult Educators*, Manchester, Department of Adult Education, University of Manchester, 1981

Candy, P., *Self Direction for Lifelong Learning: A comprehensive guide to theory and practice*, San Francisco, Jossey-Bass, 1991

Cernea, M., 'Bureaucratic Re-orientation for Participatory Rural Development', *NASPAA Working Paper*, Washington DC, National Association of Schools of Public Affairs and Administration, 1981, no.1

Cervero, M.R. and Wilson, L.A., *Planning Responsibly for Adult Education: A Guide to Negotiating Power and Interests*, San Francisco, Jossey-Bass Publishers, 1994

Champagne, A.B., Klopfer, L., & Gunstone, R.F., 'Cognitive research and the design of science instruction' in *Educational Psychologist*, 1982, vol.XVII, pp.31-51

Chow, W.T., 'Planning for Micropolitan Growth in California' in *Town Planning Review*, 1981, vol.LII, no.2

Christenson, J.A., and Jerry, W.R., *Community Development in Perspective*, Ames, Iowa State University Press, 1989

Cohen, D.W., *The Combing of History*, Chicago, University of Chicago Press, 1994

Compton, F.H., 'Community Development Theory and Practice' ed. J.A. Draper, *Citizen Participation in Canada – A Book of Readings*, Toronto, New Press, 1970, pp.382-396

Coninck, D.J., *Evaluating The Impact of NGOs in Rural Poverty Alleviation* (Uganda Country Study), London, Overseas Development Institute, Regent College, 1992

Dauncey, G., *After the Crash: The Emergence of the Rainbow Economy*, London, Marshall Pickering, 1988

Davis, M., Sorenson, D., and Walters, F., 'Industrial Development in Colorado' in *Journal of Community Development Society*, 1975, vol.VI, no.2

Deshler, D. [ed.], 'Evaluation for Program Improvement' in *New Directions for Continuing Education*, San Francisco, Jossey-Bass, 1984, no.24

Detomasi, D. [ed.], 'Toward a Generic Policy for Community Economic Vitality' (a draft paper based on the proceedings of The Four Nations Conference), University of Aberdeen, 1984

DISSA Youth Development By-Law, 1991

'Provincial Consultation and Follow-up Meeting on Community Economic Development' (draft report), British Columbia, 1992

Draper, J. [ed.], *Citizen Participation: Canada*, Toronto Press, Department of Adult Education, Ontario Institute for Studies in Education, 1971

Dykeman, F.W., 'A Return To The Past For A Community Based Planning and Action Programme For The Future – A Challenge for Planners' ed. Floyd W. Dykeman, *Integrated Rural Planning and Development*, Sackville, NB, Rural and Small Town Research and Studies Programme, Mount Allison University, 1988

Dykeman, F.W. [ed.], *Integrated Rural Planning and Development*, Sackville, NB, Rural and Small Town Research and Studies Programme, Mount Allison University, 1988

Fear, F.A., Gamm, L. and Fisher, F., 'The Technical Assistance Approach' ed. J Christenson and J. Robinson, *Community Development in Perspective*, Iowa State University Press, pp. 69-88

Fenn, W. Michael, 'Future Focus: Burlington's Strategic Success' in *Canadian Public Administration*, summer 1989, vol.XXXII, no.2

Filion, P., 'Potentials and Weaknesses of Strategic Community Development Planning: A Sudbury Case Study' in *Canadian Journal of Regional Science*, autumn 1988, vol.XI, no.3

Forsey, Helen, *Circles of Strength: Community Alternatives to Alienation*, New Society Publishers, 1993

Freire, P., *Pedagogy Of The Oppressed*, New York, Herder and Herder, 1970

Fullington, M., 'The Impact of Industry on the Economic Development of Local Communities' in *Municipal Management*, 1982, vol.V, no.2

Giroux, H.A., *Ideology, Culture, and The Process of Schooling*, Philadelphia, Temple University Press, 1981

Griffin, C., 'A Critical Perspective on Sociology and Adult Education' ed. J.M. Peters & P. Jarvis, *Adult Education: Evolution and Achievements in a Developing Field of Study,* 1991, pp.250-281

Hall, B.L., 'Research, Commitment and Action: The Role of Participatory Researchers' in *International Review of Education*, 1984, vol.XXX, pp. 289-299

Harris, W.J.A., *Comparative Adult Education*: *Practice, Purpose and Theory*, Longman, London, 1980

Head, I.L., 'Challenges to Government and to Governance', *Notes for Remarks to the Conference on Public Service and the Needs of Changing Societies*, Montebelco, Quebec, September, 1988

Higgins, D., *Urban Canada: Its Government and Politics*, Toronto, Macmillan, 1977

Hodge, G. and Qadeer, M., *Towns and Villages in Canada: The Importance of Being Unimportant*, Toronto, Butterworths, 1983

Holmes, J., 'The Atlantic Provinces' in Edward Sheffield et al., *Systems of Higher Education: Canada*, New York, International Council for Educational Development, 1978

Houle, C.O., *The Design of Education*, San Francisco, Jossey-Bass, 1972

Hume, S., 'Government Sponsored Community Development Initiatives in B.C.: 1988-1993' in *Social Development Research Programme*, Victoria, B.C., University of Victoria, 1993

Hunker, H., *Industrial Development: Concepts and Principles*, Toronto, Lexington, 1974

Ibingira, G.S.K., *The Forging of an African Nation*, New York, The Viking Press Inc., 1973

Jarvis, P., *Adult Learning in the Social Context*, London, Croom-Helm, 1987

Kauzeni, A.S., UNCRD, 'Environmental Issues: Tanzania Case' in *Sustaining Self-Reliant Local-Level Development in Eastern and Southern Africa*, Harare, Zimbabwe, 1990

Kidd, J.R., *How Adults Learn*, New York, Association Press, 1973

Knowles, M.S., *The Modern Practice of Adult Education: From Pedagogy to Andragogy*, Chicago, Associated Press/Follet, 1980

Lang, R., 'Planning for Integrated Development', ed. Floyd W. Dykeman, *Integrated Rural Planning and Development*, Sackville, NB, Rural and Small Town Research and Studies Programme, 1988

Lassey, W., *Planning in Rural Communities*, Toronto, McGraw-Hill, 1977

Lave, J. and Wenger, E., *Situated Learning: Legitimate Peripheral Participation*, Cambridge University Press, 1991, pp.12-58.

Levy, J., *Economic Development Programs for Cities and Communities*, New York, Praeger, 1981

Littrell, D.W. and Hobbs, D., 'The Self-Help Approach' ed. J. Christenson and J. Robinson, *Community Development in Perspective*, Iowa State University Press, 1989, pp.48-68.

Lotz, J., 'Does Community Development Exist?' ed. James Draper, *Citizen Participation in Canada – A Book of Readings*, Toronto, New Press, 1971, pp.118-136.

Lovett, T., 'Adult Education and Community Action' ed. Jane L. Thompson, *Adult Education for A Change*, London, Hutchinson & Co., 1980

Lynch, J., *Lifelong Education and the Preparation of Educational Personnel*, Hamburg, UNESCO Institute for Education, 1977

Malizia, E., *Local Economic Development: A Guide to Practice*, New York, Praeger, 1985

Mamdani, M., *Imperialism and Fascism in Uganda*, Nairobi, Heinemann Educational Books, 1983

Mezirow, J. [ed.], *Fostering Critical Reflection in Adulthood: A guide to Transformative and Emancipatory Learning*, San Francisco, Jossey Bass Publishers, 1990

Moron, D.E., 'Soft Tech/Hard Tech, Hi Tech/Lo Tech: A Social Movement Analysis of Appropriate Technology' ed. Gene F. Summers, *Technology and Social Change in Rural America*, Boulder, Colorado, Westview Press, 1983, pp.197-216

Museveni, Y., 'The Ten Point Programme', in *Museveni*, Entebbe, Government Press, 1985b

Nadler, L., *Designing Training Programs: The Critical Events Model*, Reading, Mass., Adission-Wesley Publishing Co., 1982

Nebbi District Development Committee Report, 1992

Nelson, L., 'The Dynamics of Rural Marketing in North-West Province of Cameroon' (Ph.D. Dissertation), University of Liverpool, 1979

Omara-Otunnu, A., *Politics and the Military in Uganda, 1890-1985*, London, Macmillan Press Ltd, 1987

Organisation for Economic Co-operation and Development (OECD), *Creating Jobs at the Local Level*, Paris, Local Initiatives for Employment Creation, 1985

Patterson, C.H., *Humanistic Education*, Englewood Cliffs, NJ, Prince-Hall, 1973

Peers, R., *Adult Education: A Comparative Study*, Routledge & Kegan Paul, 1972

Project Appraisal Memorandum (PAM) (A document submitted to the African Development Fund and the Ministry of Finance), Kampala, 1992

Peterson, J., *An Introduction to the Economic Development Planning Process*, Washington DC, US Department of Commerce, 1980

Plunkett, T. and Betts, G., *The Management of Canadian Urban Government*, Kingston, Queen's University Press, 1978

Raynor, J. and Harden, J. [eds.], 'Equality and City Schools', *Urban Education*, London, Routledge & Kegan Paul, 1973

Reinhard, L. and Summers, G., 'Changing Patterns for Community Economic Development' in *Small Town*, Ellensburg, Washington, May/June 1983

Resnick, L., 'Learning is School and Out' in *Educational Researcher*, 1987, vol.XVI, no.9, pp.13-20

Robert, C., *Managing Rural Development Ideas and Experience from East Africa*, Uppsala, Scandinavian Institute of African Studies, 1974

Roberts, H., *Community Development: Learning and Action*, University of Toronto Press, 1979

Ross, D. and Usher, P., *From the Roots Up; Economic Development as if Community Mattered*, The Canadian Council on Social Development Series, Toronto, James Lorimer & Company Publishers, 1986

Sathyamurthy, T.V., *The Political Development of Uganda, 1900-1986*, Great Britain, Gower Publishing Company, 1986

Sautoy, D.P., *The Organisation of a Community Development Programme*, London, Oxford University Press, 1962

Scott, J. and Summers, G., 'Problems in Rural Communities After Industry Arrives' ed. L. Whiting, *Rural Industrialisation: Problems and Potentials*, Iowa State University Press, 1974

Seasons, M.L., 'Economic Development in Small Communities: Current Practice and Future Approaches' ed. Floyd W. Dykeman, *Integrated Rural Planning and Development*, Sackville, NB, Rural and Small Town Research and Studies Programme, 1988

Selman, G. and Dampier, P., *The Foundations of Adult Education in Canada*, Toronto, Tompson Educational Publishing Inc., 1991

So, F., 'Strategic Planning: Reinventing the Wheel?' in *Journal of the American Planning Association*, February 1984

Sokolow, A., 'Small Town Government: The Conflict of Management Styles' in *National Civic Review*, October 1982

Sork, T.J., 'The University of British Columbia: Course materials for ADED 514, Adult Education Program Planning Theory', 1994

Southall, A.W., *Alur Society*, Cambridge, W. Heffer, 1953

Steiner, G.A., *Strategic Planning: What Every Manager Must Know*, New York, The Free Press, 1979

Stinson, A., *Canadians Participate*, Ottawa, Centre for Social Welfare Studies, Carleton University, 1979

Theobald, R., *The Rapids of Change: Social Entrepreneurship in Turbulent Times*, Indianapolis, Indiana, Knowledge Systems Inc., 1987

Thompson, J.L., *Adult Education for a Change*, London, Hutchinson & Co. Ltd., 1980

Tough, A., *Adult Learning Projects: A Fresh Approach to Theory and Practice in Adult Learning*, Toronto, OISE Press, 1979

Twaddle, M., *Kakungulu and the Creation of Uganda*, Athens, Ohio University, 1993

Tweeten, L. and Brinkman, G., *Micropolitan Development*, Ames, Iowa State University Press, 1976

Tyler, R.W., *Basic Principles of Curriculum and Instruction*, University of Chicago Press, 1949

Uma, L., *The Design of Rural Development: Lessons from Africa*, Baltimore, Md, Johns Hopkins University Press, 1975

United Nations Centre for Regional Development, *A Planning and Training Approach for Local Development in Mandang Province, Papua New Guinea*, 1992, working paper no. 92-1

United Nations Report, *Popular Participation in Development: Emerging Trends in Community Development*, 1971

Von Glasersfeld, E., 'Radical Constructivism' ed. P. Watzlawick, *The Invented Reality*, Cambridge, MA, Harvard University Press, 1984

Wade, J.L., 'Felt Needs and Anticipatory Needs: Reformulation of a Basic Community Development Principle' in *Journal of Community Development Society*, 1989, vol.XX, no.1, pp.116-123

Walker, R.J., 'Maori Adult Education' ed. R.W. Boshier, *Towards A Learning Society*, Vancouver, Learning Press, 1980, pp.101-120

Warner, P., 'Professional Community Development Roles' ed. J Christenson and Jerry Robinson, *Community Development in Perspective*, Iowa State University Press, 1989, pp.117-135

Wileden, A.F., *Community Development*, Totowa, NJ, The Bedminister Press, 1970

Williams, P., 'Community Economic Development: Coming or Going?' in *Perception*, 1987, vol.XII, no.2

Wismer, S., 'Report of the Comprehensive Examination, in partial fulfilment of the degree of Doctor of Philosophy (Regional Planning), University of Waterloo', February 17, 1986